BY SOPHIE CUNNINGHAM

graphy

lbourne (New South Publishing)

rning: The Story of Cyclone Tracy

SOPHIE CUNNINGHAM

CITY OF TREES

ESSAYS ON LIFE, DEATH & THE NEED FOR A FOREST

TEXT PUBLISHING MELBOURNE AUSTRALIA

Lines from Sappho are from Josephine Balmer's translation *Poems and Fragments* and are reprinted by permission of Bloodaxe Books.

Thanks to Magabala Books for permission to quote from *Story about Feeling* by Bill Neidjie and Keith Taylor.

textpublishing.com.au
The Text Publishing Company
Swann House
22 William Street
Melbourne Victoria 3000
Australia

First published in 2019 by The Text Publishing Company

Book design by W. H. Chong
Illustrations by the author
Typeset in 12/16 Granjon by J&M Typesetting

Printed and bound in Australia by Griffin Press, an accredited ISO/NZS 14001:2004 Environmental Management System printer

ISBN: 9781925773439 (hardback)
ISBN: 9781925774245 (ebook)

A catalogue record for this book is available from the National Library of Australia

This book is printed on paper certified against the Forest Stewardship Council® Standards. Griffin Press holds FSC chain-of-custody certification SGS-COC-005088. FSC promotes environmentally responsible, socially beneficial and economically viable management of the world's forests.

[The moon is]
                    like silver
        Sappho
FRAGMENT 112

CONTENTS

COAST LIVE OAK

COAST LIVE OAK

(Quercus agrifolia)

I saw in Louisiana a live-oak growing,
All alone stood it and the moss hung down
from the branches,
Without any companion it grew there uttering
joyous leaves of dark green

WALT WHITMAN

WRITERS love to wrestle with trees, so rich are their metaphoric possibilities, so soothing is the light that filters through their leaves. I once stood in a grove of horse chestnuts in Kew Gardens as pollen rained down through shafts of sunlight and thought to myself: ah, this is what Philip Pullman calls Dust.

Then I lay down under one particular chestnut, or rather within it, for its low boughs rested on the ground and enclosed the space and therefore me entirely, and took a nap. Trees are not good for productivity. They encourage sloth. (Also sloths, which have arms that are longer than their legs and curved feet, both features being really useful if you live in a tree.) Visiting some of the remoter trees takes time—you have to get on planes, hire cars, walk for kilometres. But I begin. I photograph trees. I walk among them. I draw them. I write about them.

The production of your average physical book takes months, which is plenty of time for an entire ecosystem to be destroyed. That knowledge should make me move faster but the effect has been quite the opposite. My photos are posted over years. I walk slowly. I write slowly. I have to teach myself how to draw. The unravelling of millions of years of evolution takes some time to wrap your head around, especially if, like me, you're still trying to come to terms with what came first: the splendour of it all.

In early 2016 I began to study painting at the Sharon Art Studio in Golden Gate Park, San Francisco. On the first day of class I posted a picture of a coast live oak that grows near there. Such was the general enthusiasm for it among my friends that I decided to commit to an Instagram feed on which I posted a picture of a tree daily: @sophtreeofday. I've only missed a couple of days since then, which means that every day I stop and look at trees and try to figure out exactly what I'm looking at.

What species is it? Should I even call it 'it'? Did it grow of its own accord or was it planted there?

I talk to them sometimes. Nap under them; and yes, I hug them.

Humans and trees share an ability to communicate. Trees release hormones and pheromones. So do we. We speak words, they pass sugars to each other using fungal filaments. You can read *relationship* in the way they grow and sway together, the way they weave around each other, the way their roots reach out to each other, the way their crowns meet overhead. The way they crowd each other out at times, and make it hard for the generations that come after them to get ahead. Some trees, like the coast live oak, like to live with a cohort and are more likely to die when separated. Other trees would rather not compete for resources and need personal space.

People like to talk about trees and to trees. Trees in cities. Trees in national parks. Since 2015 it's been possible to email thousands of Melbourne's trees directly, and more than four thousand people have taken advantage of this opportunity.[1] 'Dear Tree—If you are that big round beautiful low hanging tree I think you are my favourite tree. Such beauty on such an ugly road. Keep up the good work.' That email was sent to a golden elm on the corner of Alexandra Avenue and Punt Road and is not atypical. I don't email trees but over the last few years I've had long conversations with strangers about them, usually when I'm walking through parks.

The pleasure of tree talk is tempered by the fact that most

---

1   melbourneurbanforestvisual.com.au

days I read about, or hear about, entire populations of trees becoming endangered. We're losing trees by approximately 15 billion a year worldwide. The cedars of Lebanon are in danger from climate change. A borer is destroying North America's mountain ash, much as the elm beetle took the northern hemisphere's elms, and blight took its chestnuts. In Rome more than one-third of large old holm oaks (*Quercus ilex*) are planned for removal because of human safety concerns. Almost all the baobabs from Africa, many of them over two thousand years old, have died. Since 2010, sixty-six million trees have died in California's Sierra Nevada—contributing to catastrophic wildfire conditions. Drought has weakened trees, made them less resistant to disease or insect infestation. Within fifty to a hundred years Australia will have lost tens of millions of its large old trees. Not all of these can be replanted and those that are will take decades, if not centuries, to get to the point where they offer all the infrastructure support an old tree can provide. In tropical rainforests around the world repeated fires have killed around seventy-five per cent of large old trees and numerous intermediate-sized ones.[2]

There are parts of Europe where forests are beginning to grow again; and as the permafrost thaws and ice melts it's possible that trees will be able to colonise land further to the north and south. But historically these ebbs and flows of the climate and related ice ages have unfolded over thousands of years. Climate change is pushing this change forward in a blur

---

2 'Global Decline in Large Old Trees', David B. Lindenmayer, William F. Laurance, Jerry F. Franklin, sciencemag.com, December 6, 2012.

of speed, making it more difficult for organisms to adapt.

I too am having trouble adapting.

A tree is never just a tree. It speaks of the history of the place where it has grown or been planted: the hills that were dynamited, the creeks that were concreted, the water that has been drained to give it a place to root. Trees speak of the displacement of first nations. Of the endless lust of governments (small and large) to control places and the ways in which trees should or should not grow, the ways in which humans should or should not live.

Is a particular tree local (indigenous, native) or is it from somewhere else (exotic, invasive, introduced, a weed)? Do they belong? It's not such a complicated question when it comes to the oak that was my first #treeoftheday. Coast live oaks are unusual because they can handle sand dunes and relish the fog that rolls in off the Pacific; it hangs thick in this part of the city, especially in summer. The tree is close to one of the few remnants of oak woodlands left in San Francisco—woodlands that predate Golden Gate Park, which was developed back in 1871. Like the remnant moonah (*Melaleuca lanceolata*) on Victoria's Mornington Peninsula, these trees are dark and sinewy, they twist and turn as they dodge the winds and move towards the light. They have small leaves that knit tightly together; a delicate lacework that filters the sun.

Oaks are scattered throughout northern California, though their numbers are severely reduced. It is almost impossible now to imagine that Oakland was so called because it was thickly forested. Indeed, when I saw a photo in the

7

Oakland Museum illustrating this fact, the dissonance between Oakland then and Oakland now was such that I didn't believe the image. I wondered if it was an artwork, a fantasy, a reimagined world.

The removal of all the original oaks in the area took a few decades. At the same time, oaks were planted in the parks that were being built in both Oakland and San Francisco. (Being a native tree was a dangerous thing back then, much as being a tree that has migrated from elsewhere is now. It's hard for a tree to get it right.) Most of the people who had lived among these oaks, the Ohlone, had died under what the Spanish missionaries thought of as God's watchful eye.

You can find some magnificent coast live oak trees on the writer Jack London's estate, including one that is estimated to be between two and four hundred years old. Dying is a gradual process for a tree and untidy at times. Limbs fall; councils and insurance companies panic. The tree was to be cut down. Ann Swoveland, an elder from the Federated Indians of Graton Rancheria, blessed the tree that had provided generations of her people with acorns and inspired Jack London's writing. 'It's a beautiful tree,' she said. 'If it could talk, I'm sure it would tell many stories. We honor you.'[3]

3   'Jack London's ill oak tree gets native blessing',
Matt Brown, *Press Democrat*, August 10, 2013.

THE FALL

THE FALL

VIRGINIA and I have been married many times over, always to one another. The first time was in Brooklyn City Hall on an icy morning on February 12, 2015. As a young girl I was a romantic about marriage—I still remember the velvet and lace dress I wore to my parents' wedding—but by adulthood I was less so. We were both of us ambivalent about the meaning of the institution of marriage, as well as about marrying in a country not our own when our homeland would not recognise that marriage. We'd been together some thirteen years then and did not doubt our devotion. But still. Marriage.

So we stood in front of Waldo Ramirez, a very nice man in a pink shirt, who took us through our vows with touching respect and sincerity. Our friend and relative Rachel stood by as our witness, filming us for posterity on her iPhone. We ate breakfast bagels on the subway, went home, and got on with our working day. Low-key as the wedding was, ambivalent as we were, it had a powerful effect. It reinforced our commitment to each other. It changed people's reactions to us. In my experience people are less homophobic if they can find a way into understanding your relationship, and in America our being married gave people that way in. Once I was married I started to understand just what was being denied to all people in same-sex relationships, to anyone who is told by the state that they are not due the full opportunities and protections of the law. I was grateful to the United States for giving me that right.

I first visited that country in 1967, too young to remember much more than helium balloons in the shape of Mickey Mouse; Cocoa Krispies in a breakfast diner; modular furniture in a daycare centre in Boston. My most recent trip was in the second year of the Trump presidency, 2018. In 2015 and 2016 I lived in the Mission district of San Francisco, around the corner from Balmy Alley, a laneway famous for its murals. One particularly striking mural, by Janet Braun-Reinitz, depicts some of the horror of the AIDS epidemic and incorporates a line from the Yeats poem 'The Second Coming'. *Things fall apart; the centre cannot hold; / Mere anarchy is loosed upon the world*. It's impossible not to see the truth in this. The centre is failing, and we're left to maintain traction in the chaos. Or perhaps the situation is this: we're falling off a cliff in slow motion. Me, I grab at the trees I see on the way down in an effort to break the fall. I look at what I see around me as I tumble, for I want to remember it all—the landscapes, the animals that may not survive the impact.

When I moved to San Francisco I knew the whole Summer of Love vibe was over. Joan Didion had told me so in her essay, named for the same Yeats poem as Braun-Reinitz's: 'Slouching Towards Bethlehem'. The San Francisco she described in 1967 'was a country of bankruptcy notices and public-auction announcements and commonplace reports of casual killings and misplaced children and abandoned homes and vandals who misspelled even the four-letter words they scrawled'.[1] She stepped over starving, tripping children in the Haight.

Fifty years later I zigzag to avoid stepping in human shit, walk through tent cities, see people dozing off with needles hanging out of their arms, sit on the bus next to people: smoking ice, cursing faggots, screaming at each other, smashing their phones and falling apart in all the ways a human possibly can. I walk under the 101 and give thanks

---

1   'Slouching Towards Bethlehem', *Slouching Towards Bethlehem*, Joan Didion, p. 84.

that the rottweilers barking at me are tethered near their owners' tents. I catch a glimpse of a pretty teenage girl in a tent on Folsom Street brushing her hair and my heart rises to my throat: what will happen to her? I learn that waking up to gunshots is an injection of adrenaline direct to the heart.

It's not all bad—it never is. The tacos and chilaquilas in this town are so good they can move a person to tears. We walk to Japan Town on the weekends for a hot or cold Japanese bath, a movie. We visit the Saint John Coltrane Church and listen to 'A Love Supreme'. We eat really good bread from Tartine and The Mill, and shop at the almost fifty-year-old Rainbow Food Co-op.

The city's history of social progressiveness is not just hype: San Francisco has been home to bohemians, LGBTQI folk, artists, immigrants and activists for more than a hundred years. But here are some fun facts. New York has the largest population of homeless people, but the homeless of Los Angeles have the least access to shelter. San Francisco has the largest number of ultrarich (people worth more than 30 million dollars) in the country, while the state of California has the worst poverty rate in America. Confusingly, San Francisco's complex history includes unionised workers, radical activism and more infrastructure for supporting the disenfranchised than exists elsewhere. It's a relatively small place: only 884,000 inhabitants who live in low-density housing on a peninsula of 120 square kilometres. For all these reasons the gulf between rich and poor is particularly visible and particularly intense and the pressure on the city's real estate is ferocious. When I moved to the Mission the Latino population were being forced out by newcomers like me who were able to pay higher rates. 'It's a war zone here,' said Mission resident Paula Tejeda[2] when she described the clash between older residents and newer ones.

Long-term residents, many of them poor, live alongside a vibrant bar and restaurant scene. The gang presence was an excuse for all kinds of police brutality, including an incident that hung like a pall over the district: the murder of the young Latino man Alex Nieto on Bernal Heights in 2014. People go up to Bernal Heights to hang out, to walk their dogs. Nieto was there one evening, sitting on a bench and eating a burrito. He was on his way to work—dressed for his job as a security guard at the El Toro nightclub, and carrying a licensed taser. During the day Nieto was a scholarship student at Community College San Francisco, studying for a criminal justice degree, and was a member of various community groups including the Mission Peace Collaborative. Some witnesses say he was behaving erratically, others deny that was the case. Police were called by a dog walker who didn't like the look of him. A report by the District Attorney showed that fifty-nine bullets were fired, fourteen or fifteen of which hit him. He was twenty-eight years old. The police who were responsible for that shooting were not indicted.

From a distance Bernal looks like something out of the opening credits of a television series. It's a high, bare hill, with only a few trees on the top of it. There is something about

---

2 'Gentrification Spreads an Upheaval in San Francisco's Mission District', Carol Pogash, *New York Times*, May 22, 2015.

the perspective up there that means you can see the details of individuals walking their dogs: the owner leaning into the wind, the dog leaning away from the leash. You can look across the Mission and down Broadway to San Francisco Bay. You can watch the fog (named Karl) do his crazy rush up and through the cleavage in Twin Peaks, snaking down through Noe Valley and the Castro and stopping a few streets away from where we lived in the flat lands. One morning, after being shimmied out of bed by a minor earthquake, I decided we needed an earthquake plan. I hung an embroidered bag on the door with two pairs of underpants, photocopies of our passports, a pair of scissors and a garbage bag. I kept meaning to add a water bottle to the kit but I never did. We decided that if we were apart when the earthquake hit we'd head to the top of Bernal Heights in the hope of meeting up. Bedrock.

On June 26, 2015, just after we moved to San Francisco, the Supreme Court made a ruling enshrining the fundamental right of same-sex couples to marry in all states in the US. The ruling coincided with San Francisco Pride. By way of celebration an established Latino gallery, Galeria de La Raza, installed a temporary mural, 'Por Vida', on the corner of Bryant and 24th streets. San Francisco is home to about three thousand murals and most of them are in the Mission. This particular work, by Manuel Paul, a Chicano artist from LA, celebrated gay pride in three panels: in the first, two men embrace; in the second, a trans man wears his surgical scars with pride; in the third, two women gaze into each other's eyes.

All the faces depicted were Latino or Latina. I walked past the mural most days. It was, over a period of some weeks, defaced three times. The gallery's staff were repeatedly threatened by locals who objected to the mural. The issue was not just homophobia, but the belief that the focus on the right to sexual equality was related to the gentrification process. There was also an objection about the appropriation of traditional *cholo* art for a work about queer love. The gallery's director, Ani Rivera, pointed out that queer Latinos have always lived in the Mission: 'Some think this level of sexual liberty is associated with a level of—a sort of—privilege. They keep saying, "Go to the Castro." Well, we've never been in the Castro…It's not a new trend we're starting. It's part of that cultural history and legacy.'

Each time the mural was painted over or slashed, the gallery replaced it. But on June 29, 2015, following Pride weekend, the mural was set on fire, which put the entire building at risk. A celebration of the mural and a protest over its destruction was held in Bryant Street two days after the fire. At least two hundred people turned up. A group of women did a traditional Aztec dance. For peace, they said.

Virginia and I went on a belated honeymoon a few months later and headed south to New Orleans. When Hurricane Katrina hit that city in 2005 the turmoil in the Gulf of Mexico led to a revelation: a bald cypress forest that had been submerged for more than fifty thousand years. The wood, when cut, still smelled of cypress sap and when we visited the

Honey Island Swamp in Louisiana we smelled that same scent. Rust-coloured fronds of cypress in autumn swayed overhead as we moved through the waterways in our small boat. Cypress can live for more than a thousand years and, while they can't live permanently in water, they can tolerate it for long periods. As we looked into the swamp we saw knotted stumps sitting above the waterline. They look much like the aerial roots of mangroves but bigger and knobblier, and are consequently known as 'knees'. It used to be thought these knees provided oxygen when the swamps were in flood, but now scientists assume they work as a form of structural support, along with the buttress bases on the trunks. The buttresses, the knees and a strong, intertwined root system allow bald cypress to resist strong winds—which is lucky, as they've been hit with plenty of those.

In 2017 the states along the Atlantic Ocean and the Gulf of Mexico were struck by some seventeen hurricanes, the most deadly of which were Hurricane Irma and Hurricane Harvey. Category 5 hurricanes formed an orderly queue in the North Atlantic before taking turns to slam into Cuba, the Virgin Islands, Puerto Rico and Florida. It was one of the deadliest hurricane seasons on record and certainly the most expensive. (These words come up a lot: worst, hottest, wettest, dryest, coldest.) The hurricanes prompted the then mayor of Miami, Republican Tomás Regalado, to say that it was time 'that the President and the E.P.A. and whoever makes decisions needs to talk about climate change'. A hard call in a state where the then governor, Rick Scott, also a Republican, had instructed state workers not even to use the term. State employees were supposed to speak instead of 'nuisance flooding'. Call it what you like. Being tricksy with language isn't going to change what is happening now, and what will happen next.

Although tolerant of water, bald cypress (*Taxodium distichum*) don't like salt, and when we visited wetlands in the Ninth Ward of New Orleans, most of the cypress had died: poisoned slowly after navigation channels were dug in the eighteenth century to join Lake Pontchartrain to the Mississippi. The channels are rarely used these days and have slowly fallen into disuse, but they have continued to contribute to regular flooding.

After Louisiana we headed to Miami to drive down the Florida Keys—islands so narrow that in parts they were nothing but a sandbank lined with feral iguanas. We were heading down to see Ernest Hemingway's six-toed cats, which proved to have, as advertised, six toes. We squinted south in hopes of seeing Cuba. And because it was our honeymoon, there was an evening where we sat by the water at Islamorada and looked across to the floating green fields—sometimes described as rivers of grass—of the Everglades National Park.

At the end of that month the *New Yorker* published an article by Elizabeth Kolbert. 'The same features that now make South Florida so vulnerable—its flatness, its high water table, its heavy rains—are the features that brought the Everglades into being,' she wrote. It's not so much a wetland as a slow-moving river system that once spread out over three million hectares. Now one in every three Floridians relies on it

19

for fresh water. The area is home to seventy-three endangered species including the American alligator, the Florida panther and the manatee, though I suppose they weren't endangered back in 1845 when the embryonic state of Florida began to drain it. Now the water is becoming salty, the sawgrass is in retreat and mangroves are moving in. As of December 12, 2018 the Trump administration had unveiled a plan to weaken rules intended to protect the wetlands and streams nationwide from pesticide runoff, imperilling this area further.

Endless media reports about the death of the region do not prepare you for the vibrancy and beauty of this vanishing place. We drove up to Miami Beach and that too was more lovely and strange than I'd been prepared for. And even more expensive—it's hard to exaggerate how much money is dug into these thirty-nine square kilometres, in real estate alone. A penthouse on Miami Beach can cost you 35 million dollars. We rode bikes from the mix of natural and human-made islands that make up Miami Beach across to Miami itself, then back again, through water that was spilling over gutters and onto roads and footpaths.

Sunny-day flooding occurs when salt water rises up through the limestone that underpins most of South Florida. It's most likely to happen at high tide. Half a billion dollars has been spent in recent years in an attempt to alleviate the problem. Footpaths have been elevated, pumps installed… Stopgap stuff. These aren't long-term solutions.

On one of our nights there we walked along the Miami Boardwalk alongside hundreds of feral beach cats. The cat colony dates to the early 1900s, when the city's first mayor shipped them in to deal with the rats. Soon, in a scenario wearily familiar to Australians, the rats were gone but the cats stayed. And multiplied. We were walking down to eat at the famous Joe's Stone Crab, a restaurant that sits on Miami Beach's southernmost point. Going there is a step into the proverbial Hot Tub Time Machine where you're whisked back to a heyday that never existed. You wouldn't be surprised to see a young Frank Sinatra sitting at the bar. You order martinis. Shaken, stirred; dry and dirty. 'I feel sometimes like we're in Normandy in 1944,' said Stephen Sawitz, the fourth-generation owner of the restaurant, when asked about the frequency of the flooding. 'Where is the invasion going to come? Calais? Omaha Beach?'

Kolbert's article talked about the irreversible decline of the West Antarctic Ice Sheet. A segment of the sheet, known as the Amundsen Sea sector, contains enough water to raise global sea levels by more than a metre and to trigger the melting of other parts of the ice sheet, which would add three more metres. This has happened before, she points out, twenty thousand years ago, at which point so much more water was frozen that sea levels were almost 120 metres lower than they are today and Miami Beach sat twenty-five kilometres off the Atlantic coast.

> Beginning around 12,500 BC, during an event known as meltwater pulse 1A, sea levels rose by roughly fifty feet in three or four centuries, a rate of more than

21

a foot per decade. Meltwater pulse 1A, along with pulses 1B, 1C, and 1D, was, most probably, the result of ice-sheet collapse. One after another, the enormous glaciers disintegrated and dumped their contents into the oceans. It's been speculated—though the evidence is sketchy—that a sudden flooding of the Black Sea toward the end of meltwater pulse 1C, around seventy-five hundred years ago, inspired the deluge story in Genesis.

These floods pulsed on for thousands of years. Closer to my home town of Melbourne, Port Phillip Bay was a grassy plain until only a thousand years ago and the people who lived there, the Boon Wurrung, still remember the sudden influx of seawater. The deluge took only a matter of days but it triggered long-term crisis and chaos.

The daily high-water mark in the Miami area has been rising at the rate of almost 2.5 centimetres a year, nearly ten times the rate of average global sea-level rise.[3] Storms and associated heavy rainfall are increasing. The attempts to drain the Everglades and associated engineering works have made things worse. At the risk of oversimplifying things, it's fair to say that wetlands act as a sponge—absorbing and contracting as needed, as varying amounts of water move through the system—and when they can't do that, you get floods. The region may have less than half a century before it goes under.

---

3 'Letter from Florida: The Siege of Miami' Elizabeth Kolbert, *New Yorker*, December 21 & 28, 2015.

Before white settlement Melbourne was also a watery place, with expanses of swampland alongside grasslands and open forests. It's no Everglades, but the CBD of my home town sits on top of a water catchment the size of about 150 football fields. Elizabeth Stream (also known as Townend Creek, Williams Creek and Enscoe) once ran through a valley, which became known as Elizabeth Street. That street became a drain as the vegetation that fringed the margins of streams was stripped away. It turned the natural beauty of the Elizabeth Street valley into what one observer described as 'a brawling impassable torrent in winter and snake-haunted gully in summer'.[4] A series of stepping stones that were the remnants of volcanic eruptions some 800,000 years ago formed a natural crossing of the Yarra at what we now know as Queens Bridge, and this natural bridge was known to early settlers as the Falls. It was the Falls that had determined the site for the city's foundation: they formed a barrier between the brackish tidal water downstream and the fresh water upstream. Water moving down the river and over the Falls had carved a saltwater basin below them large enough for ships to dock and turn. But the boats couldn't pass the natural barrier and above the Falls punts were used.

'In the earliest days of Melbourne's settlement, as in the period before Europeans arrived, people crossed the river on much the same line as Queens Bridge now lies. But what kept their feet dry then was not a bridge but a ledge of rock that

---

4   *The Place for a Village*, Gary Presland, Museum Victoria Publishing, 2008, p. 87.

spanned the river.'[5] William Buckley crossed there in 1803, decades before Melbourne existed, on the run from the convict colony that existed briefly at Sullivan Bay in Sorrento. The Falls were finally removed in the 1880s during the construction of Queens Bridge—at which point the salt water moved up as far as Dights Falls and poisoned the city's water supply.

So much engineering has gone into shifting Melbourne's waterways, into excavating canals, rerouting rivers and building freeways that float above drains that were once chains of ponds. There is no going back to the landscape that was once here but—despite concerted effort—the waterways that fed into Elizabeth Stream have not been totally erased: they've just been driven deep underground. The watery places that snake and seep around and through this place we now call Melbourne are still with us; as they are still with those who live in Florida, and in the swathes of San Francisco that have been built—sometimes using rubble from the 1906 earthquake— on what were once coastal sand dunes. Our home in the Mission was reclaimed wetland built over the Mission Creek: long submerged, though it still bursts out from time to time, sending water rushing into the doorways of the businesses along Folsom and driving the homeless from their tents.

The eighteen months after our return to Australia were not made easier by the endless debates about our right to marry, which seemed to devolve into the right of LGBTQI teachers to teach and the right of bakers to refuse the supply of wedding

---

5   Presland, p. 19.

cakes. My daily postings of #treeoftheday, always a salve, had not offset the creeping distress caused by the 'debate' around equal marriage. I had found my still point in this turning world—my marriage—only to have it attacked. I found having my private life talked about so publicly in this fashion quite excruciating. There were about a million of us directly affected by the debate. As a middle-class white woman I was, perhaps, naive or entitled or both. I found politicians' concern to monitor their citizens' sexual and emotional lives perplexing. For the most part it was white, older men insisting that it was their job to monitor and manage our lives for us. We were to be told WHAT TO DO. We were to be told WHO WE ARE. That we were instructed in these things by politicians incapable of developing a sustainable energy policy, or any other legislation that might help Australia and the world face the threat of climate change, further eroded my respect for them.

On December 10, 2016 our Australian friends, frustrated and saddened by the government's ongoing refusal to allow our right to marry (and their right to party) threw us a surprise wedding. One minute Virginia and I were walking through the streets of Fitzroy to dinner with a couple of friends on a Saturday night, the next minute we were in the midst of a group of people that divided around us so we were effectively walking down an aisle. It was extraordinary how long it took me to get what was going on. Why was there a hot pink laser-cut perspex sign hanging from the roof saying *Ginny & Soph*? Was it a coincidence that Matt, who loves pink and owns a laser cutter, was filming us? Why were most of the small children I knew throwing confetti at me and looking so excited? What were my mother, old school friends, dear new friends, and our neighbours doing drinking together in a bar on a random Saturday night? Why were all these people staring at us, cheering, smiling and crying, dressed in party finery? What strange coincidence was this that our friend Carolyn, who is a cake-making genius, stood next to a two-tiered coconut shag cake decorated with grevillea? Then we got it, burst into tears and cried for approximately the next five hours.

On November 15, 2017 our marriage was finally recognised. It had been a hard few months. Thousands of us—young and old, and by no means all queer—congregated around Trades Hall in Lygon Street. The line to get into the party went for several blocks. Some of us shook the then opposition leader Bill Shorten's hand before moving on to the more serious business of drinking, hugging and dancing. It was sweaty, hot and, by my increasingly staid and middle-aged standards, wild. Clothing was removed. Strangers were pushed together into a mob that jumped up and down on the spot singing. It was a joyous, riotous, primal scream of FUCK YOU to a government that chose to throw the LGBTQI community, along with millennials, new immigrants, refugees and the entire planet, to the dogs for the purposes of power and profit.

Earlier that day, the day that the postal vote on equal marriage was counted, Virginia was working in San Francisco and I was walking through the Carlton Gardens on my way to the forecourt at the State Library of Victoria where the crowds were gathering. Virginia called me and we were both surprised by how emotional we were feeling. What if the vote didn't go our way? I arrived at the library forecourt and found friends standing near the statue of Governor La Trobe and his ridiculous hat. At 10 a.m. the Australian Statistician, David Kalisch, slowly, diligently, took us through the results. 'It's probably the only time millions of Australians will gather to hear from the Australian Statistician,' he said, and it's fair to say that David was enjoying his moment in the sun. He talked for a few minutes longer than perhaps the agonised crowd found ideal. I struggled to hear him through the distortion of the speakers.

Seventy-nine point five per cent of the eligible population had voted. I heard that. A hush descended that made what followed clearer still. '*Yes* responses—7,817,247, representing 61.6 per cent of clear responses. That's 61.6 per cent of clear responses were *yes*.'

Waldo may have been our first celebrant; David was our last. I do. We did. Married. *Yes*.

GIANT SEQUOIA

GIANT SEQUOIA

(Sequoiadendron giganteum)

The branches beneath the wound, no matter
how situated, seem to be excited, like a colony
of bees that have lost their queen, and become
anxious to repair the damage.

JOHN MUIR

IANT sequoia are among the world's oldest trees. They
lived with the Mono and the Washoe people for
millennia. They witnessed the arrival of the Spanish
and then settler Americans who'd travelled across the
continent in the early nineteenth century. They were
there when California became a state (1850) and the land

31

they'd taken root in became a national park (1890). Forty-five different American presidents have officiated on their watch, imposing their various views regarding the logging of the giant sequoia's kin. They're too tall to see to the top of; far too wide to hug; much bigger than blue whales.

I tell you all this but it doesn't convey their impact. I struggle to think what would. When I walked through a grove of them tears streamed down my face. I found myself thinking, I would lay down my life for you, then left the need for language behind. Is this why they're so hard to write about?

Richard Powers' Booker-shortlisted novel *The Overstory* is one of the few things I've read that begins to convey how being in the presence of giant sequoia is like being in the presence of qualities Christianity ascribes to God. There are individual giant sequoia (*Sequoiadendron giganteum*) still living that are older than Buddhism, Islam, Christianity, Judaism. If one of these trees started a religion, that is the religion I would join. They have such presence that as you walk among them you find yourself imagining they might uproot themselves and walk to higher, more expansive ground. They make anything seem possible.

But it's not.

Redwood's early relatives appeared in fossils that date back 100 million years and spread from Northern Mexico and the Canadian Arctic to England. During the late Miocene, some 10 to 20 million years ago, the closest direct ancestor of the giant sequoia lived in what is now southern Idaho and western Nevada. As the Sierra Nevada Mountain Range continued its uplift and the climate became drier, the giants' range shrank. Today, the last remaining sequoias are limited to seventy-five groves scattered along a narrow belt of the western Sierra Nevada.[1] There are multiple challenges for the giant sequoia. Temperatures are now too high for them, even at higher altitudes. Once considered drought resistant, they have begun to die during times of drought. They have only 144 square kilometres to call their own and that area is broken up into scattered groves. This fragmentation is one of the greatest threats to old trees and the ecosystems they support. It leaves them far more vulnerable to disease, the vagaries of weather and fire. The size of giant sequoia also presents them with problems. A small area can only support so many giants, but they have no new habitat to expand into. According to biologist David Lindenmayer and his colleagues, large old trees are predicted to disappear from California, Costa Rica and Spain within ninety to 180 years. In southeastern Australia we'll have lost more than ninety-eight per cent of our large old trees within fifty to a hundred years. That includes *Eucalyptus regnans*, better known as mountain ash, the earth's tallest flowering plant. Brazil's fragmented rainforests have already lost half their original large trees.[2]

Most systems of law and governance place human beings at the centre, and view humans as separate from nature, but in recent decades environmentalists and lawyers have begun to work out a way of framing a holistic approach to law and

1   'Giants in the Face of Drought', Thayer Walker, *Atlantic*, November 27, 2016.

2   Lindenmayer et al., 2012.

governance: wild law. Rights for nature were first proposed by Christopher Stone in his 1972 article (later a book) 'Should trees have standing?' That same year the Sierra Club took the Disney corporation to court in an attempt to block their plans to build a ski resort inside the Sequoia National Park. While the courts rejected the lawsuit, the case prompted a famous dissent by Justice William O. Douglas, who accepted Stone's argument that trees should have the legal right to sue for their own protection.[3] This would give them the same legal rights as humans, and is known as personhood.

But trees—particularly giant sequoia—can live for centuries and millennia; laws come and go. And as humans develop systems of thought to support the environment, corporations are fighting back and long-accepted environmental laws are struggling. For example: in the US the Endangered Species Act of 1973 legislated species' rights to exist. It was that law that saved the condor and the wolf, if saved they are. It is that law that Republican lawmakers, lobbyists and the Trump administration now seek to amend or, worse, overturn.

In his book *Drawing a Tree* Bruno Manari tells me to look at the roots of trees closely, before looking at the trunk, and then at the patterns of their branching. Last of all he exhorts me to look at the shape of the individual leaves and consider the way in which they do (or don't) cluster. Diligent, I look.

---

3   'It's only natural: the push to give rivers, mountains and forests legal rights', Jane Gleeson-White, *Guardian*, April 1, 2018.

Roots. Can you trace the patterns they make under the soil? Are they buttress roots, high as a house, or is the root system deep underground, mirroring the tree's crown? And what about the sound of them? The first thing you hear when a giant sequoia falls is a series of low booms as the roots snap, one at a time. In Dunn's Woods, on the campus of Indiana University, I became fascinated by a crackling sound, a kind of electric hum that rose out of the earth when I walked through the trees. At first I thought it was insects in the dry leaves or squirrels digging for acorns, but soon I became convinced I could hear the seedlings as they pushed up, rustling the dry leaves that had fallen during the winter. And yes, scientists can detect these sounds, and roots do make tiny clicking noises, though at a frequency of 220 hertz, they are supposedly inaudible to humans.

Trunks are more fun still. Shagbark hickory looks like a cross between dreadlocks and roof shingles. Shaggy, but not as shaggy as an Australian ribbon gum, which sheds in long narrow strips to reveal paler, smoother bark underneath. Giant sequoia trunks are as tall as a skyscraper and can have a girth of eight metres. A paperbark has hundreds of papery slices of bark, compressed together, fine as filo pastry, to form a papery slab you could use for shelter. Bloodwoods ooze hard red sap and smell pungent after rain. Scribbly gums are named for the tunnels of the moth larvae that live between layers of bark and career around like drunken street racers until, as the top layer of bark falls, the trunk is revealed as a scroll.

Bark demands to be touched if you are to get its measure,

and the most extraordinary bark I've felt is, of course, that of the giant sequoia. It's fire resistant. It's spongy, and up to a metre thick. Its alternating slabs and furrows are themselves the width of 'ordinary' trees . If you lean into it hard enough it enfolds you, so I did that when I was walking through the Giant Forest sequoia grove. I leaned against one and felt it give. Stroked it. Then, concerned I was being weird, I stopped and sat down under it for a while. That's when I saw the marmots dash past, fatter and more hilarious than I'd been capable of imagining. That is when I heard the insistent tap-tap-tap of the woodpeckers.

Leaves. Don't get me started. The natural variation within a species can be great. Juvenile and mature leaves are often different. In my attempts to understand leaves and therefore taxonomy, I come across this word: systematics. Systematics is, I read, a way of understanding the evolutionary history of life on earth.

How to tell the difference between pine, fir, spruce, cedar and cypress? That was another challenge. Research suggested that if the number of needles coming out of the same spot was two, three or five, it was a pine. If there was only one needle it was a fir or spruce. Then you need to pluck the needle: if it is soft and doesn't roll easily, it's a fir. If it has four distinct sides and is stiff, which makes it easy to roll, it is a spruce. And so on.

I can't tell you a lot about a giant sequoia's leaves, to be honest: they sit so high in the sky it's hard to make out the leafing patterns, let alone the shape of the individual leaves. I had to go to the internet to discover that as many as two billion leaves (evergreen, awl-shaped) arrange themselves spirally on shoots. To learn that an established leaf can live for up to twenty years, drawing water up the tree's trunk and sending nutrients down it, while the trunk amasses wood. Giant sequoias' leaves are responsive to, and cope well with, environmental changes but, this being California, pollution levels are increasingly challenging. The management of the Sequoia and Kings Canyon national parks tweet daily air-quality advisories.

The individual branches that support the spiralling leaves are often the size of large trees and it is these branches and their leaves that make up the crown: wild and raggedy cities some thirty metres across that sit higher above the ground than a thirty-storey building. The crown is wiry. There are tufts. You can see the remnants of crowns that have been sheared off by storms.

I'm so far away from having the skills or the patience to draw a giant sequoia accurately that for a time I don't even try. Instead I try to capture the redwood's glow and the abruptness of its crown—a kind of bowl cut maintained by major weather events. More important is the matter of perspective. I sit in front of a trunk about five times as wide as my body, close enough to consider the variety of tones in its charcoaled interior—the tree I've chosen has a chamber near its base first opened out by wildfire then polished, by time, to a small wooden cathedral. The red huskiness of the bark becomes an entire page of blocked colour with a core of charcoal black. My sketch barely makes it above the root line.

I visit the giant sequoia in June 2018, but after my return to Australia I can't stop thinking about them and the ways in which I might convey how *transporting* they are. Or is this what I want to convey: giant sequoia *transform* the meaning of things?

I try again, using my square notebook. Hopeless. I buy a rectangular one, but the dimensions continue to be too modest. I get closer to capturing the crown's raggedy charm, but my attempt to convey its height by whittling it to a point fails dismally. For this is another thing about the giant sequoia. They do not look narrow up higher. Perhaps this is to do with the fact that you can't take in the width at the base of the tree unless you look at it from a distance. Then, once you do walk away, the tree starts to look more ordinary. Jon Mooallem wrote in the *New York Times* about the way the human eye wants to 'find a way to correct for the sequoias' unacceptable gigantism', flattening perspective 'so that, say, four far-off sequoias appear to be right alongside six cedars in the foreground—fusing all of them into a single line of ten perfectly boring-size trees.'[4]

Despite the seeming impossibility of it all, I continue my consideration. My reading about, writing about, and drawing of the tree. I move between abstract and more practical considerations. I dig out a handmade paper concertina four times as long as it is wide and I draw the sequoia in a more considered way. I do not radically narrow the trunk but simply let the base of the tree slip off the side, thereby leaving its

---

4 'In the Land of the Giants', Jon Mooallem, *New York Times*, March 23, 2017.

width to the imagination. I resist the impulse to make the tree look elegant but make sure to include gashes and boules. I draw small cartoony pines in the background. I hint at other sequoias. All of this helps. Next I try to find a larger piece of paper, one that is dramatically longer than it is wide and that will take charcoal and pastel. I end up with a compromise, which is to cut a large sheet of paper into two. It isn't quite right and it is hard enough to manage that I have to hang it from the clothesline to work on it. This time I capture the red glow but not much else. I get out of bed one morning, pull out a second sheet of irregular-shaped paper and start again. The colours of my first tree are too garish. I've failed to convey its height. The second attempt is better on those points, but the crown still isn't working. And so it goes. It's become clear to me that there is no getting it right. Even clearer: that isn't the point. I have another plan. Is it possible to draw, or write, a forest?

STAYING WITH THE TROUBLE

STAYING WITH THE TROUBLE

THESE essays are all over the place: the United States, Australia, Europe, South America and Iceland. My twenty-teens have been a peripatetic time but there have been constants. Trees was one of them. Walking another.

At the end of 2013, on the morning of my fiftieth birthday, I was in Paris. I woke up early and went outside;

it was the day after Christmas and the light was deep indigo: an intense morning twilight that lasted for almost two hours. This half-light, morning and evening, is my favourite time. A hovering between action and inaction. Between potential and limitation. Like ocean swimming on a cloudy day: the seafloor corrugating below, looming and receding as the depth changes. Like walking through a thickly treed forest under a heavy canopy on a sunny day. When my friend Georgia Blain titled her final novel *Between a Wolf and a Dog*, I learned that the French had a phrase for this light: *L'heure entre chien et loup*.

It was very cold when I arrived in New York a couple of months later. Some temperature I couldn't decipher because it was measured in Fahrenheit. A wind tunnel had formed around the taxi queue at JFK and I was almost blown over. The trees were stark against the sky. But within two, maybe three weeks, in what seemed like the blink of an eye the trees that lined the city streets were in full blossom. In another blink, spring was almost over, and by the time I visited the cherry grove at Brooklyn Botanic Garden a month after I arrived, petals were raining down, carpeting the ground in shades of lavender and pink.

A month before I moved to that city my stepdad, who I thought of as Dad, had moved back to Melbourne from Indonesia. He and I had spent decades doing that: living in other countries, rarely crossing over. On the day he moved back to Australia my brother flew in from Canberra, I drove in from Fitzroy and we met Dad and his exhausted wife at the airport and took him to a high-care dementia ward in Flemington. He was quite cheerful when we left him that first time but things unravelled over the next few visits. Soon he was begging us not to leave him there, to please take him away. Anywhere: to the south coast of New South Wales, Bali, Lygon Street. I was called into the manager's office because the staff had questions. They found Dad stressful. I was surprised that they were surprised.

Things got worse, of course they did, far worse. It would be disrespectful to Dad to detail the ways. But his descent, when it came, was dizzying, even by the standards of such a place. I learned phrases I'd never heard before, like 'chemical restraint'. I argued with doctors about the point of treating his weak heart to keep him alive. Suffice to say a time came when I looked at Dad, sixty-eight years old, snarling in a wheelchair, pulling against his straps and cursing, over and over, at the top of his voice. I reached towards him and he hit me. The word 'hit' seems a bit harsh; he was a lot lighter than me, something I couldn't get used to, given how heavy he'd once been. I pulled my chair out of reach of his and waited for him to feel better, but that did not happen. I will never forget this. His deep distress. His terrible rage. Somewhere in among all this I tried to remind him that I was living in another country for a while but would be back in three months to spend time with him.

Three months. What even is that?

He looked at me and started to cry.

Said, 'So that's it?'

Percy Grainger walked to avoid the temptation of self-flagellation. David Sedaris walked to placate his Fitbit.

Virginia Woolf walked the streets of London and later the South Downs endlessly: because she loved it, because she was walking her dogs, because she needed to think clearly. For Henry Thoreau, every walk was a sort of 'crusade'. Sarah Marquis, who walked sixteen thousand kilometres over three years, sought a return to an essential self. 'You become what nature needs you to be: this wild thing.'[1] For James Bradley it can be an evocation, a provocation, 'any walk was also an act of remembrance, the web of connections associated with each house or street recalled as we passed it.'[2] Will Self began walking after he gave up heroin, though in his novel *Walking to Hollywood* (2010) the protagonist walks not to escape addiction but because he fears he has Alzheimer's. This feels familiar. My brother and I had first been introduced to the pleasures of walking by Dad; in the seventies he'd taken us on lots of hikes—most memorably to Wilsons Promontory. But these days my brother joked about starting a group called Running Away from Dementia. Sometimes, catching sight of my posture reflected as I walked around New York, I wondered if I was doing the same thing. Walking away from fate. If so, could one ever walk fast enough?

After several months in New York, during which time I'd returned to Melbourne just the once, some friends and I chose to walk the extent of Broadway. We started at a point on the tip of Manhattan that was once a village called Marble

1   Elizabeth Weil, 'The Woman Who Walked 10,000 Miles (No Exaggeration) in Three Years', *New York Times*, 25 September 2014.

2   'An Ocean and an Instant', James Bradley, *Sydney Review of Books*, August 21, 2018.

Hill. At the end of the nineteenth century a shipping canal was tucked in behind its southern edge, rendering the tiny town an island in the Harlem River. Nine years later, with a flourish of landfill, it was attached again, this time to the northern mainland—a vestige of Manhattan annexed to the Bronx. Small facts like this delight me.

I don't know who built the Broadway Bridge, which links Marble Hill to its old stomping ground, but Native Americans worked on many of the bridges and skyscrapers of New York: 'sky walkers', they were called. Our walking was more prosaic: eight Australians, one of them male; all bookish types. We met under the bridge before heading over it, southwards to Inwood. It is green up there, and the large park that sits between the Hudson and Broadway rises steeply from the street. Among its tall trees are remnants of Manhattan's original forests; in its swamps the original salt marshes. The bald eagle, a species that has clawed its way back from 'endangered' status to merely 'threatened', has been rereleased into the park after more than a hundred years of absence.

I'd only been to Inwood once before, one hot Sunday afternoon. Music blared from cars and shops; we ate shaved ice standing on a street corner. This day was colder, quieter. It was fall, sunny, ten degrees. The weather here turns on a dime, was already moving, swiftly, towards a new season. By the time we reached Battery Point eight hours later, it would feel like winter. We had much ground to cover, so we moved quickly, passing the incongruous Dyckman Farmhouse museum without much more than a glance. Built in 1794, it sat small, low, out of time, surrounded by a cottage garden; looking across to a gas station and a gymnasium.

Walking is often a solitary activity, but on this day it was gloriously social. Conversation ebbed and flowed as the eight of us moved between one another and talked. It was like a slow, elaborate dance. Judy and I discussed our feet at some length. Do they wear out with age? It was a question that had been on my mind as both the necessity and pleasure of walking New York's streets had taken its toll. Around Washington Heights, Francesca and I talked about parents. She had lost one of hers to dementia as I was losing Dad. It's not just Dad, I told her. Other people close to me also have dementia, or have died of it. I didn't tell her I was having violent dreams. That my memory failed me. That I became lost for words. That I'd been to my doctor to discuss my fear—phobia might be a better word—that I was getting dementia, and the doctor said, 'It's probably just stress. Or menopause. Or both.'

Francesca and I discussed what it was like to witness such unravelling, and wondered what it was like to experience it. As if to answer our question, leaves flew around in the wind. There was a scattering, a loss of coherence.

The sun moved up, then overhead, to the west. By the time we walked through Times Square, it had disappeared behind the skyscrapers. Deep in the canyons of the city, the wind whipped up the avenue. We moved past lumbering humans dressed as Muppets and superheroes. By now we were in single file; talking had ceased. Walt Whitman's description of Broadway as 'unspeakable' suddenly felt apt.

Ten or so blocks later, Virginia took a photograph of us crossing the road to Madison Square Garden, Francesca striding out in front, Persephone-like. We rested in the park. Squirrels scampered over us, looking for food. Donica fed them nuts. The squirrels' audacity revived us temporarily, but by SoHo we were cold and tired again. Lucy, tiny and compact, looked as if she might simply keel over. My feet throbbed in their boots. The pavement made everything harder, more jarring. People crowded the streets in a buzz about the beauty of the streetscape, excited by the weight of their huge shopping bags. We were by now immune to such pleasures, driven to get this insane venture over with. It was around 6 p.m., near the Wall Street Bull, when we arrived at Number One. We could see the water and, yes, the Statue of Liberty. We had walked close to thirty kilometres. 'Didn't you say it was only going to be twenty-one?' someone asked me. I had. I'd been wrong. No matter. We cheered, took photos for Instagram, and then headed towards a pub on Stone Street, one of the first roads to be paved in Manhattan.

Two days after our walk along Broadway, my yoga teacher decided that the time had come to discuss the articulation of the feet: specifically, drawing up from the arches to activate your legs, mobilise your core. 'You see,' she said, 'you do this.' She moved her foot almost imperceptibly, just enough that I could see tiny muscles ripple as she planted it firmly on the ground before stretching herself. She stood taller, lighter—not quite in the league of Menuhin conducting Beethoven's Fifth with his feet while standing on his head, but still impressive.

'As a literary structure, the recounted walk encourages digression and association,' Rebecca Solnit writes in *Wanderlust: A History of Walking*.[3] It is true that one of the common uses of walking is to permit the writer a meandering narrative. But should digressions be allowed when walking? A few weeks later, on an even colder walk, the question came alive. Sure, an obscure pizza place on Avenue J that makes *The Best Pizza in New York* might only be a few blocks off Flatbush, but if we had dedicated ourselves to a day of coming to know Flatbush Avenue, was it legitimate to seek experiences outside it?

'The blogs I have read,' I declared authoritatively, 'say that if you plan to walk the full extent of an avenue you should not step off the path. That is not in the spirit of the walk.' The day already promised a carousel in Prospect Park, Caribbean curry, old-style diners, theatres and the high school where both Barbra Streisand and Neil Diamond were educated. Wouldn't it be greedy to expect more?

I am not a consistent person. My rule, within seconds of its announcement, was challenged by happenstance. As we walked towards the Flatlands Reformed Church—built on the site of a Native American village in 1654 and therefore a goal of sorts—I realised it was off Flatbush. I hesitated momentarily, then turned left onto Alton Place. It was worth it. A plaque in the church gardens told us lots of things, including the fact that George Washington had ridden this road in April 1790. On the same plaque there was a reference to Indian braves, but not to the village that had once been there. A woman offered to

---

3   Rebecca Solnit, *Wanderlust: A History of Walking*, Penguin Books, 2001.

show us around the church, a simple white, wooden building. Once inside, I looked up at an ordinary painted ceiling that bore no adornment of any kind, then to the balcony at the back of the church. 'That's where the slaves sat,' the woman, who was African American herself, told us.

We retraced our steps and turned left onto Flatbush. To our disappointment, it was not long before the avenue was eight lanes wide and lined with shopping malls. All charm vanished. It was tempting to give up, especially as no one seemed to know where the original Flatbush began or ended. But we chose not to be churlish and kept going. Suddenly, to our left, there was a coastal channel lined with houses, their balconies hanging low over the water. Mill Basin. It was only 3 p.m., but the light was pearly-grey, moving towards the pink of sunset. Seabirds circled in large numbers. We walked a bit further and saw a pier jutting out into the water, lined with petrol pumps. Virginia stood for a moment then said, 'This looks like Metung.' She was right. How strange to feel echoes of the Gippsland Lakes here in the most populated borough of New York. That has been one of the wonders of Brooklyn. There is so much nature here, albeit nature that is struggling to hold its own.

Horseshoe crabs are prehistoric creatures that look much as they did half a billion years ago, which means that they are known as living fossils. During their breeding season they used to line the beaches of the eastern coast of the North American continent in their millions. Their spawn sustained whole populations of birds, most notably the wader known as red knot. They can still be found on Brooklyn's beaches today. When I first visited them, I had been so starved of the beach that a rush of surprise and relief sprang to my eyes. Unexpected tears. The sea. Open sky. A narrow stretch of sand. It was windy and grey, but it wasn't cold. There were windsurfers and, in the distance, factories. Feral cats prowled the low-lying dunes. I had signed up as a volunteer to count mating pairs of the crabs.

Our business was to keep track of the horseshoe crab's numbers so that they could officially be listed as endangered, a status that might afford them some legal protection. The crabs used to thrive on the shores, but today the numbers are modest. An immodest number—half a million or so— are hung up each year in labs and partially drained of their blood, which, once processed and made into a product called Lysate, enables the identification of bacteria in particular pharmaceutical products. The pale blue liquid sells for fifteen thousand dollars a litre. After being bled, about fifty thousand or so crabs each year flat-out die. The rest are returned to the ocean where they 'fail to thrive' and drift around half-dead, too weak to breed. There are claims that some labs don't even bother to return living crabs to the ocean, but just sell them as fishing bait. I'm not sure which is worse, though: the use of such ancient creatures for fishing bait strikes me as appalling in the same way as cutting down old-growth forests to make pulp. Contemptuous in a way I find hard to process. Before pharmaceutical companies discovered the horseshoe crab, they used to be harvested by the million for fertiliser.

Horseshoe crabs, to be clear, have survived multiple major ice ages and the end-Permian mass extinction 250 million years ago. They were indulging in group sex on the beach—much as I was witnessing on my first evening among them—back when the dinosaurs were roaming. Did dinosaurs roam the beaches? I do not know. I do know this: when mating, the male crabs attach themselves to the females with their 'claspers', which are small claws, and then ride out the waves so they can get to smooth sand. If they make it to the shoreline, they secure themselves by digging into the sand before getting down to business. Often a female crab will have several male crabs attached to her.

Here are some other things I know about horseshoe crabs. They live for decades; they have nine eyes scattered about (on their shell, beside their mouth); the Nobel Prize in Medicine was awarded in 1967 in part for research performed on the horseshoe crab eye. I know the females are startlingly large—as much as sixty centimetres in length—but no amount of research, no photo, could have prepared me for the awesomeness—I use the word in the old-fashioned sense—of these creatures. They look like thickset barnacled dark-brown dinner plates circa 1970, the retro style of hand-hewn pottery that was back in fashion. I fell in love with the crabs immediately. I picked one up, using two hands and grasping either side of its large shell. She flailed at me all the while, using her claws and legs like spears. I got the message and put her down.

We picked them up in pairs and brought them in to measure and tag. When we did so, the male would hover close to the female, though one lone guy wandered off in the other direction, cueing gags about a lack of chemistry. The tagging involved drilling a small hole in the corner of their shells, and sometimes the pale-blue blood that makes them so valuable spurted out, translucent. I would plug the hole up quickly with a plastic tag, worried that I had hurt them. I don't make any claim to know if the crabs feel pain, or think what we'd call thoughts. I wondered, as they rode out the waves of a beach off Brooklyn, were they aware of the industrial city pressing down upon them? Did they notice that the tide was high? That the water temperature was eighteen degrees (we measured it) and the air outside a bit cooler? Or that a full moon was rising? They must have had some instinct for all this, for it was the sea temperature, the tide and the moon that were bringing them together.

There are six companies with crab-bleeding facilities in the United States. They stand to lose a lot of money if artificially produced Lysate (developed by a scientist named Jeak Ling Ding some fifteen years ago and known as Factor C) becomes widely available.[4] Some companies, such as Eli Lily, however, have become concerned that crab-bleeding will be restricted in future and realised they need to move on. By 2018 it seemed that some companies were finally prepared to start using the artificial product.

When I spoke of my concerns about the fate of the

---

4 'The Last Days of the Blue-Blood Harvest', Sarah Zhang, *Atlantic*, May 9, 2018.

horseshoe crab at a writers festival back in 2015, before any respite was on the horizon, Antony Loewenstein, an activist and writer whom I know and admire, asked me to explain my interest. He wasn't trying to be rude, he said; he just found my concern so random. We are in the midst of the sixth extinction, living, as political scientist Audra Mitchell puts it, through 'an unmaking of being'.[5] More than half our biodiversity was destroyed between 1970 and 2010 and the losses are increasing at a precipitous rate. The rate of extinction is faster than it was when the dinosaurs disappeared. Why focus on these barnacled dinner plates? Why not elephants and tigers, wolves and dingoes? Giant sequoia or mountain ash? Why not Leadbeater's possum? The regent honeyeater? Orange-bellied parrot? Bees? Frogs? Dragonflies?

Random. The word interests me. As I get older, I no longer try to find meaning in order so much as draw meaning from randomness. I feel this strongly: things are both random and connected, all the time. Leonard Woolf used to say 'nothing matters', by which he meant 'everything matters'. All of it. The lot.

Not long after Antony's question, my friend Helen emailed me to say her grandson had asked her to suggest something 'random' he could draw. Helen had said to him, 'I've just read a book about Cyclone Tracy. A lady said she looked out and saw dogs sailing through the air with their chains still on.' Her grandson agreed, 'Yes, that is random,'

---

5 'Extinction: A Matter of Life and Death?', *The Philosopher's Zone*, ABC, November 21, 2014.

then produced a drawing of doubled-over palm trees with chooks and dogs flying.

So we talked about this word, Helen and I. She had found a description of it as 'the latest buzzword used among mindless teenagers as a way of showing just how utterly irreverent their predictable sense of humour is'. That seemed harsh. To us, the word's usage meant something closer to 'weird and not particularly logical'. Helen asked her grandson what he meant by the word. The eight-year-old gave the question some thought before saying, 'It's hard to give a definition of a word without using the word itself.'

On the last day of fall, a group of us walked Brooklyn's longest avenue: Bedford. It took us from the serenity of the white swans circling at Sheepshead Bay, past kilometres of family homes and dog-walking locals, Brooklyn College and multiple high schools. In the morning, the sun was shining, but in the afternoon the day took on a greyer cast. We walked through what was once known as Automotive Row and past the now-abandoned Studebaker showroom. We walked through Crown Heights and Bed-Stuy. We walked into South Williamsburg, home to many of New York's Hasidic Jews. We did not feel welcome there and walked purposely, swiftly, to indicate we did not mean to intrude upon the neighbourhood. It was a shock to arrive at the divide between South Williamsburg and the north, a border so clear it was if we had arrived in another country, a country full of bikes and bike lanes, bars and street art. Of all the walks we did, this was the one where gentrification, rampant or resisted, was most apparent. Brooklyn has become one of the least affordable places to live in America.

It would be nice to make some theoretical claim here (many have) that meandering walks represent the creative process. But you could walk forever and not end up with words on a page. That doesn't seem so terrible to me. I listen to politicians engage in rhetoric, semantics and blatant lies. I attempt to use language to describe various concerns, and fall into apocalyptic cliché. Dad, sitting in a nursing home losing words by the day, was yet another reminder of the ways in which language can fail us. It is images I turn to: a hundred-year-old photo of a man standing atop a pile of bison corpses; Pacific islanders trying to sweep the rising sea from their homes; California on fire. I begin to paint and draw.

Around the time we did the Broadway walk, an article from the *Washington Post* described American psychologist Martin Seligman's experiments of 1967.

He put a dog into a box with two chambers divided by a barrier that could be jumped over. When one chamber became electrified, the dog ran around frantically, finally scrambling over the barrier to escape the shock. In later trials, evading the shock becomes easier and easier for the animal until it would just stand next to the barrier, waiting to jump. But the outcome is much more grim if a dog first learns that electric shocks are uncontrollable and unavoidable. If animals were repeatedly shocked while tied up beforehand, then later placed in the same box free to roam, most didn't jump the barrier. Instead, they lay down whining and took the jolt. Subsequent trials confirmed the animals' same passive, defeatist response.[6]

These experiments seem horrendous to me, and the lesson obvious: helplessness can be learnt. The published findings went on to inform CIA interrogation techniques.

So: walking. We walk to get to one place from another, but in doing so we insist that what lies between our point of departure and our destination is important. We create connection. We pay attention to detail, and these details plant us firmly in the day, in the present. They bond us to place, to people. Walking opens our hearts. Thoughts stop swirling in tight circles. They loosen up. Meander. Slow down.

New York City has invited people to walk its streets for hundreds of years. Anthony Trollope, Charles Dickens, Walt Whitman and Herman Melville not only walked New York's streets, they also wrote about them, as many have done since—as I am trying to do. More recently, William B. Helmreich, a sixty-eight-year-old professor of sociology at CUNY, walked almost every street in New York City: 120,000 blocks, or about

---

6   'Why Are Some Depressed, Others Resilient? Scientists Home in on One Part of the Brain', Meeri Kim, *Washington Post*, June 5, 2014.

ten thousand kilometres.[7] In Teju Cole's first novel, *Open City*, walking the streets of New York appears, at first, to be an expression of engagement and curiosity for Julius, a Nigerian psychiatrist who wants to embrace his new home. Julius's walks lead to a series of pronouncements and observations: on the flocking of birds, on failed relationships, on race, on class and on history. But Julius's digressions take on a bitter edge. Random observations and the rambling narrative structure that sustain them become attempts to erase the past, a past that includes a mistreatment of women. A meditation on gender is not where I intended to go, but it is certainly one of the places Cole does. Sometimes there seems to be no way of escaping it, even when all you want to do is walk or read about walking. It was when doing the latter that I noticed this casual aside from *The Art of Wandering*, that the walker 'remains, despite notable exceptions, predominantly male'.[8]

I compare this bald statement with Rebecca Solnit's exploration in *Wanderlust* of the ways in which women are discouraged from walking, the oft-cited concerns for safety that are motivated by a desire for control. She goes onto posit that 'Black men nowadays are seen as working-class women were a century ago: as a criminal category when in public.' As I read her, I have a memory of a midnight walk one hot summer night, pacing down the middle of Nicholson Street, arms flung wide for no reason other than joy at being alive, the freedom

---

7   William B. Helmreich, *The New York Nobody Knows: Walking 6000 Miles in the City*, Princeton University Press, 2013.

8   Merlin Coverley, *The Art of Wandering: The Writer as Walker*, Old Castle Books, 2012.

of walking without scrutiny. A privilege.

Walking provides an excellent opportunity to argue with people in your head, so I argue with Merlin Coverley, the author of that aside. I imagine telling him about Australia's Sorrel Wilby, who trekked through the Himalayas in 1991, wrote about that experience, and has been walking ever since; of Lisa Dempster's 1200-kilometre walk through Japan and her book, *Neon Pilgrim* (2009). I remind him of Robyn Davidson's extraordinary 3000-kilometre pilgrimage through Australia's deserts, enshrined in *Tracks* (1980), of Cheryl Strayed's hike from Mexico to Canada, the subject of her bestseller *Wild* (2012). Coverley, I say, do you not know of Charlotte Brontë and her creation Jane Eyre? 'I'll walk where my own nature would be leading. It vexes me to choose another guide.' Of Jane Austen's *Pride and Prejudice*, whose heroine Elizabeth Bennet walks everywhere, often unescorted, much to everyone's consternation?' 'I do not wish to avoid the walk,' she insists. 'The distance is nothing when one has a motive; only three miles. I shall be back by dinner.'

My preoccupations collide in unexpected ways when I return from such a walk, and listen to a podcast on philosophy and extinction. In it the Australian environmental philosopher Thom van Dooren quotes a line from the feminist theorist Donna Haraway: 'We need to "stay with the trouble".'[9] She went on to publish a book with that title in 2016.

Walkers stay with the trouble. The Situationists called their walks *dérives* to distinguish between the unconscious

---

9 'Extinction', *The Philosopher's Zone*, 2014,

act of strolling and their more politically charged way of moving through Parisian streets. Women march to reclaim the night. Between 1863 and 1881, William Barak, an elder of the Wurundjeri clan of the Woiwurrung people, walked the sixty kilometres from the Coranderrk Estate to the steps of Parliament House some three times: to call for his people to be paid for their labour; to seek the right for his people to have their own community; to insist on their freedom to keep their children within that community. A hundred years later, during the civil rights marches, African Americans attempted the eighty-seven kilometre walk from Selma to Montgomery on three occasions, despite the brutality of the beatings dealt out to them. Here in New York, fifty years on, people were walking the streets, crossing the bridges, outraged by the fact that policeman Daniel Pantaleo was not to stand trial for the choking of African American Eric Garner. 'I can't breathe,' Garner gasped as he was suffocated. 'I can't breathe.' Breathing becomes harder and harder. There is so much trouble to stay with. Can we, like Thoreau, make every walk a 'crusade', a reclamation of our cities, our lives, our land, our planet?

As you move through history, history moves into you, more surely than if you read it. Writers mark the page, but walkers mark the earth, and the earth in turn marks us. I feel increasingly compelled to walk to random places, to know them through the soles of my feet. I am keener and keener to look into the eyes of animals that aren't human. (What do they see when you look at them? Well. That is a whole other question.) But when I think of the horseshoe crabs I'm clear that my attachment to them isn't entirely random. In their plight I recognise our own. It is not just the crabs that are being left to float aimlessly in ruined seas. It is not just the dogs we live with, poison, walk with, experiment upon, that are left to whine; to take the jolt.

GINKGO

GINKGO

(Ginkgo biloba)

The time comes when you know that, if you plant a
tree in your garden, you will not be alive
to stand beneath its branches.

LEONARD WOOLF

THERE used to be two ginkgo trees, a male and a female,
growing on either side of the entrance to the Geology
Department on the Parkville campus of Melbourne
University. Only the female survives today. It is recorded
on the City of Melbourne's Exceptional Tree Register.
I've also met a ginkgo in Tavistock Square, London.

That was planted on December 16, 2004, to commemorate the centenary of Leonard Woolf's arrival in Ceylon. I visited the tree because I was writing about Woolf, though I'd been much more aware of his love of elms and apple trees. He had two elms, one named Leonard and one named Virginia. His apple orchard at Monk's House is full of hand-grafted and heritage trees that he laboured over for decades. So this ginkgo business, this was a surprise to me.

Ginkgo were, for some millennia of their long existence, confined to China, but now they live around the world. They have fan-shaped leaves that turn gold in autumn. They're considered sacred in several Buddhist traditions and are cultivated in and around temples. It's believed that the spiritual company the ginkgo kept was the reason it survived near-extinction. Ginkgo thrived in the Jurassic period, but the ice ages that came thereafter were hard on it. Luckily humans fell in love with the ginkgo and began to cultivate it. Slowly the tree found its way out from China back to the land masses it lived on some millions of years ago.

I was delighted, in Brooklyn, to see ginkgo all around me. Until autumn approached and I started to notice the smell of vomit everywhere. At first I assumed that humans were the problem—they usually are—but then I learned that it was the seed of the female ginkgo: a smell so strong that it's speculated that it evolved to attract dinosaurs.

Many claims are made for the ginkgo. The internet tells me that an extract from the leaves 'seems to improve blood circulation, which might help the brain, eyes, ears, and legs function better. It may act as an antioxidant to slow down Alzheimer's disease and interfere with changes in the brain that might cause problems with thinking'. Male ginkgo, like cycads and ferns, produce sperm that actually swim. The trees are known as living fossils because they are the only one of their division, Ginkgophyta, to have survived and because they have changed so little over 200 million years that you can recognise them in the fossil record. A Shinan ship that sank in Quanzhou Bay in 1323 and was excavated in the mid-1970s was carrying not only a priceless cargo of porcelain, but also botanical specimens that included a single ginkgo seed. Antarctic explorer Robert F. Scott had ginkgo fossils on him when he died. In 1829 John Phillips published a two-volume treatise on Yorkshire geology, which included a list of fossils on the Yorkshire coast. Among these was a widespread Jurassic species that was, it turned out, the first fossil ginkgo discovered. However, despite a lineage that cuts through several geological ages, the ginkgo was not named until 1712 and even then the name we use today is thought to be the result of a misspelling of gin kyo.

Ginkgo were among the top ten trees to be found in New York City in 2015, the last time a tree census was done—there are about 21,000 of them. They're not great for native fauna, though the eastern grey squirrel does eat the nuts. Survivors, selfish, they don't pull their weight in the urban forest. An urban oak may provide habitat for more than five hundred species of caterpillar, a ginkgo might host only two. That means fewer birds, fewer animals. Before 2007 the boroughs that make up New York, New York, drew their street trees from a list of about forty species. These days they're planting some 220, though some of these are struggling. The research is thin and various, but I read any number of articles claiming such trees were lucky to live ten years. The term 'useful life expectancy' of trees is one estimate used by arboriculturalists. It can be controversial as it's a subjective assessment of the tree's health, not an objective calculation. Some advocates for retention of European trees argue that ULE is being used as a justification to remove trees and replace them with native species. The most accurate reckoning I could find of the lifespan of street trees in big cities in North America was nineteen to twenty-eight years.[1] And here is the thing about ginkgos: they are tough. The reason they have survived 200 million years is that gingko can handle most things you throw at them, which includes staying alive for centuries in urban environments. They were planted in nineteenth-century London because they could survive the terrible smog. In New York they endure poor light, pollution, vandals, meagre soil and, occasionally, being hit by trucks. They resist disease and fire. They are cheap to run because they have a branch structure that makes them easy to prune. Biodiversity issues aside, the smell is really the only thing counting against them. For a while cities around the world tried to deal with this by planting male trees, but it can be decades before it's clear what sex a tree is, so that didn't work either.

*

1   'How Many Trees Are Enough? Tree Death and the Urban Canopy', Lara A. Roman, *Scenario 04: Building the Urban Forest*, Spring, 2014.

Akihiro Takahashi was a schoolboy when an atomic bomb was dropped on Hiroshima. He survived, horribly scarred, and by 1984 he was the director of the Hiroshima Peace Memorial Museum. When the novelist Ariel Dorfman met Takahashi he described his body as 'a testament to that war crime and its aftermath. One ear was flat and mangled, his hands were gnarled, and from a finger on each grew a black fingernail'. After a long conversation Takahashi said to him, 'You must see the *hibakujumoku*, the survivor trees. You must see the ginkgos.'[2]

Six ginkgo planted in Hiroshima survived the nuclear blast of August 6, 1945 and are still alive today. Their bark was scorched and some were deformed, but they grew new shoots and buds the very first spring after they were nuked. It was their deep roots, apparently, that allowed them to survive the blast, making their green shoots the first signs of new life in that ravaged city. As the city rose out of its ruins, temples were rebuilt to accommodate the ginkgo.

Sir Peter Crane, the author of *Ginkgo: The Tree that Time Forgot*,[3] has spoken of the message inherent in the ginkgo's existence. Not just ancient of lineage, individual ginkgo reach a great age. They teach us to think in longer increments of time, Crane suggests. They challenge us to think outside election cycles and human life spans: to encompass a notion of existence with roots that reach into the depths of prehistory, with branches that can reach out to a similarly expansive future.

---

2 'The Whispering Leaves of the Hiroshima Ginkgo Trees', Ariel Dorfman, *New York Times*, August 4, 2017.

3 *Ginkgo: The Tree that Time Forgot*, Sir Peter Crane, Yale University Press, 2013.

TOURISTS GO HOME

TOURISTS GO HOME

CLOSE to nine million people visit Barcelona a year, and the permanent population of 2.5 million are sick of it. Residents of the old city are being pushed out—by the expense, the crowds (people like me) and the noise. *Tourists Go Home* is sprayed on walls and pavements. It's harder and harder to find a place on the planet where the locals don't want you to fuck off and go home. (More to the point, it's harder and harder for people on the planet to find a home at all.) Countries around the world are beginning to cap the number of tourists allowed to visit significant sites.

When I visited Barcelona in 2013, tensions past, present and future were rising to the surface. Literally—as the graves of thousands of Franco's victims were being unearthed by archaeologists in woods around Catalonia. Plaça de Vicenç Martorell, not far from our hotel, was home to nomads— perhaps they were Romani—who had no home, or jobs, and were, as far as I could gather, walking around Europe with their dogs and backpacks. They were young, dreadlocked, magnificent, trying to take charge in a world that had to all intents and purposes abandoned them. The youth unemployment rate in Spain at this time was close to fifty per cent. One afternoon I sat and watched police circle these kids. Go through their back packs. Threaten them. It's okay to be a traveller if you have money, it seems, but less acceptable if you don't.

I started travelling whenever I had the chance, by which I mean cash, after my grandmother died and left me a small amount of money. That money stretched to a few weeks in Europe and a few months in India and Nepal. A gift. Later in my twenties, my travelling intersected with my professional life. I wrote travel articles, researched my novels and, when I worked in publishing, I visited publishers and book fairs. For a short while these interests coalesced when I worked at

Lonely Planet, the publishing house that specialised in travel. More recently my wife Virginia's work life has contributed to the travel miles. From 2013–16 we lived in the US.

Over the decades I started to ask myself more questions. What does it mean to visit a city, a place, a landscape that is changing beyond recognition because of geo-political chaos, population explosion and climate change? To visit a country where there is extreme poverty? To visit a country where there is extreme wealth? I made decisions not to visit particular places on political grounds—by which I mean over and above how the politics affected my personal safety—but it's fair to say that until very recently I loved travel so much that it never occurred to me *not* to travel; or to prioritise earning a living, saving and superannuation, over a trip.

I've been told that talking about all this travelling risks making me seem obnoxious. But when I first went overseas in the early eighties it was becoming a generational rite of passage. In 1971, Qantas acquired its first Boeing 747-400 and tripled the number of people that could be carried on an individual flight from one to three hundred. To *not* travel spoke of timidity, smugness, lack of curiosity; though clearly one can exhibit those personal qualities while being on the move constantly. Travelling on a tiny budget was part of the test though I can only (now) imagine what a strain it is to manage an endless stream of anxious, broke young adults turning up on your doorstep.

The numbers of Australians travelling just keep increasing and these days more than 10 million Australians head overseas to work and holiday each year. At the end of the nineteenth century the rich were appalled by the appearance of travel companies like Thomas Cook that specialised in providing tours to the middle classes. The jostling for a higher position in the pecking order has continued since then, and no small percentage of tourists like to think of themselves as 'real' travellers. It's all a bit beside the point in the face of the numbers—an estimated 1.2 billion people travel each year. And while I don't like to think that I am obnoxious, tourism's effects undoubtably are, and not just because of the carbon footprint left by all that plane travel.

Let me give you an example. The finches that helped give birth to Darwin's theory of evolution are in danger of extinction: both a distressing reality and an awful metaphor. In 2007 the Galápagos were listed as a 'worldwide heritage in danger'. These islands are home to Darwin's finches, a group of fifteen species that were observed by Charles Darwin in the 1830s. The finches, specifically their beaks, contributed to his groundbreaking work *On the Origin of Species*. More recently a team of scientists have identified a gene that explains variation in beak shape within and among species. The finch's common ancestor arrived on the Galápagos about two million years ago. Since then they've evolved into species that differ in body size, beak shape, song and feeding behaviour. Changes in the size and form of the beak have allowed them to eat food as diverse as insects, seeds, nectar from cactus flowers and blood from iguanas. These finch species are now threatened, and some have become extinct. Most endangered of all is the mangrove finch, which is now confined to three small mangrove swamps on Isabela Island. There are only around a hundred birds left. This drastic ecological change has been fuelled, in part, by the rise in tourism from 40,000 visitors in 1990 to more than 200,000 in 2015, a year in which the local population was only 30,000. The tourists include 500 introduced animals and 700 plant species, and they too are causing a severe impact on the native biodiversity.

In October 2014 I walked part of the Inca Trail in Peru with friends. On the second day the trail took us over two 4000-metre passes, a series of (for me) extreme ascents and descents. The first of these was called Dead Woman's Pass. This was something to do with the silhouettes the mountains form, though as I trudged slowly uphill it felt more ominous than that. The issue wasn't just physical fitness, but altitude. I chewed on dried coca leaves, which reminded me of oregano that'd been sitting at the back of a cupboard for ten years. I stood, vague, wobbly, by the edge of a cliff, and contemplated lying down to sleep. Finally a guide poured some oil from a small bottle and rubbed it into his hands before cupping them over my face. He told me to breathe deeply, and when I did I felt a sudden burst of enthusiasm. I was later unsurprised to be informed that the oil could not be taken out of the country. When I asked what it was made of the guide told me, with a smirk, condor wee; but given how rare condors are we both knew that wasn't true. They're in danger of extinction for all the usual reasons. Loss of habitat, hunting, competition for resources from humans, pesticides.

Andean condors mate for life. The males hold their wings aloft to dance when they are trying to impress a potential mate; they hiss and cluck while the skin on their neck turns bright yellow and inflates. They have a wingspan of close to three metres and they can use those magnificent wings to ride thermals for hours with only the occasional flap. To be honest I wouldn't have minded if the oil had been made of condor wee, I was just very keen to get my hands on some more of it, so cheerful did it make me, so fleeting was the high.

When I got to an Incan ruin after about nine hours of oil-free walking and saw there was another hour to go before we reached our camp, I cried and swore. ('I loved it when you said, "Fuck this for a joke,"' an Irishwoman in our group enthused.) Of course the pain quickly receded, and what I remember now is: vertical gardens hanging from sheer cliffs, forests with their canopies in the clouds, hummingbirds so tiny that at first I thought they were colourful bumblebees, orchids growing between the cracks of stones in abandoned ruins and terraces, breathtaking in their scale, stepping their way down the Andes.

At first, ruins seem picturesque, but the more of them you walk over the more the specific details grab you. I found myself wondering how the massive granite boulders were carved so particularly. We asked, and were told that cold water was poured into natural fissures when the boulders were hot from sitting in the sun. This would cause the cracks to widen so that wedges could be inserted, and over time the rocks would split.

How long would it take to build a city in this fashion? Not so long, apparently. Maybe ten years.

While I walked leadenly through the rain carrying a small daypack, porters sprinted past me with bulky loads strapped to their backs. I wore boots, they wore thongs. Only ten years ago it was usual for these men to carry loads of fifty kilograms or more, to be poorly fed, extremely underpaid and not provided with shelter. Things are supposed to have improved, with some companies fined for overloading and underfeeding their porters; but it was hard to get a fix on how much better their conditions have really become. They were so speedy it was not a stretch to imagine the young messengers known as chasquis who ran relays barefoot across what are now several countries.

I asked our guide if the Incans had a written language. He became frustrated as he answered me, because the ways in which his ancestors communicated were not recognised as language. This is one of the reasons the devastation of the Inca is not well documented, though it's believed that after the Spanish invaded Peru in the mid-sixteenth century the Incan population was reduced from an estimated 10 million people to 1.5 million. The surviving population was enslaved, their culture and language banned. My guide explained that the chasquis carried 'talking knots': string arranged like a necklace with knotted strands that look like macramé. Because the knots didn't relate directly to spoken language, the Spanish were quick to ban them on the grounds they could not interpret them. The Incas could, in effect, talk about them behind their backs.

On our last morning we got up at 3 a.m. to arrive at Machu Picchu. This was partly so we could get there as close to dawn as possible, and in part to avoid other tourists, who numbered upwards of 2500 a day, despite efforts made to reduce them. Machu Picchu was never intended for mass habitation. Built around 1450 for the Incan emperor Pachacuti, it is in fact not so much a city as an estate. Now the millions of visitors have unwittingly led to Machu Picchu, like the condor, being classified as endangered: a UNESCO world heritage site in danger of being trampled to death by the numbers who visit it.

I didn't think of that as I walked, so effortful was the journey. Then I stood at the Sun Gate and looked down upon Machu Picchu and all the popular stories came to life: *Raiders of the Lost Ark*, Tintin in *Prisoners of the Sun*. Grey stone buildings and terraces sat against vivid green jungle in the clefts of several mountains. The precision of the layout reflected sophisticated agricultural and irrigation systems, nuanced astrological understandings. Houses were a mix of the humble and the grand, alongside temples dedicated to the sun, the moon and the condor. It was a shock to realise that, despite such impeccable planning, the estate was inhabited for only a century before it emptied out and was claimed for several hundred years by the forest. Not because it was discovered, nor because it was attacked. It was smallpox—introduced by the Spanish—that destroyed much of the population.

On our last day in Peru we walked around Saqsaywaman, a ruined settlement above Cusco. Monumental boulders too heavy for colonists to remove and use for other purposes formed the base of walls that jutted this way and that for hundreds of metres. Some said the zigzag represented lightning bolts, others that the walls suggested a puma's teeth. I walked across a plain to the hill opposite to decide for myself. As I stood there, I tried not to think of the Andean condors that had had their wings savagely clipped, nor the de-clawed pumas we'd seen at an animal rescue centre earlier that day. The walls, I decided, were lightning bolts, but it was hard to get a proper perspective. In Incan constellations, as in Indigenous Australian ones, animals are found in the negative space: the black between the stars. When the Incas first saw the Spanish, they believed they were part-human, part-animal because they arrived on horseback and the man and horse were seen as one creature. I carry these ideas with me: that there is meaning in the space between, that we and the creatures that carry us are one.

I joined the throngs once more that year, this time at the Grand Canyon, which has around five million visitors a year. I first visited in the early nineties and I'll never forget the moment of getting out of the car in a bog-standard carpark and walking towards the north rim. Despite the canyon's size—more than five thousand square kilometres—it comes upon you suddenly as you approach the edge and look down into this extraordinary ravine that plunges deep into the earth. It was late afternoon and the canyon walls were adorned with striated purples. The rocks and the light—it was hard to distinguish one from the other—shifted from grey to lilac to dark purple to black. The visit was so brief that when I left the next day it was as if I'd dreamt it. The sign at the gate warned us there would be no refund if weather conditions precluded a good view. Virginia and I looked at each other. Did people really do that? Demand refunds if the canyon didn't display its extraordinary dimensions, its dramatic shifts of light? Apparently so.

This trip we planned to hike down into the canyon, something I hadn't had the time to do on that first brief visit. Only one per cent of the canyon's visitors ever make it below the rim and each year around 250 of those need to be rescued. Worse still, a not inconsiderable number of them die: the average over the not-quite-a-century the park has existed is twelve people a year. It's easy to see how this happens. If you're not an experienced walker you'd be hard pressed to imagine how demanding the descent to the river and the return will be. You won't know what it's like to bake in temperatures as high as 49 degrees Celsius, or how much drinking water you'll need. Signs everywhere warn against overconfidence in your own endurance. The same signs discourage you from hiking from rim to river and back again in a single day, which is the undertaking most likely to result in heat exhaustion. I'd read reports of Spanish explorers in 1540 who returned after several hours having covered only a third of the distance to the river, reporting that 'what seemed easy from above was not so'. They were correct, both in their assessment of difficulty and in pointing out that it was hard to get perspective on the matter. The descent (and ascent) along the trail is so sheer that you can't see what's in store for you when you look down from above.

The trail we chose was the popular Bright Angel Trail, which a much younger, fitter friend had told me was 'kind of challenging'. This was alarming to my old ears. There we were. Four adults, two kids under thirteen. The first part of the walk, down to Indian Gardens, was easy enough and the zigzag of paths, the sheer walls of the canyon, the mule trains, were hypnotic. The day was cool. The gardens, when we got to them, were an oasis, sitting on what you first think is the floor of the canyon until you realise you are still four hundred metres above it as the crow plummets. Cottonwood trees lined the creek and leaves glittered gold, brown and pale yellow in the autumn light. The grass was green and the harshness of the canyon's sheer walls faded away.

In 1928 the Native Americans living in Indian Gardens, the Havasupai, were told to move to the reservation at the bottom of the canyon, an area eight kilometres long and twenty kilometres wide. Curtailing their seasonal migrations between the canyon floor and the plateau above created enormous difficulty for them, and at one point government-restricted boundaries had taken away nearly ninety per cent of their land. In 1975, 185,000 acres (75,000 hectares) was returned to them. National parks are on land that is taken, at the government's pleasure, from the indigenous people who have lived there for millennia. The intention is to protect nature in perpetuity and preserve that landscape for the pleasure of tourists. We've been given, or perhaps I should say we've stolen, a gift. (Australia's Kakadu National Park was the first national park in the world to talk of protecting 'living culture' and to prioritise the relationship between human custodians and the land. Since the late 1970s Kakadu's traditional owners have leased their land to the Director of National Parks and continue to jointly manage that land.)

After Indian Gardens the walk became easier and we walked through flatlands populated with thousands of purple cacti. The bright, direct light of midday flattened everything out. We walked in silence. Time stretched out. Walking on and down into a landscape bonds you to place. Even if—especially if?—that walk includes an eight-kilometre hike back up the canyon during which you ascend close to a kilometre; an incline that at first leaves you cursing but soon reduces you to speechlessness. Over the eight hours it took to walk only twenty kilometres, we became sensitive to the moods and light of the canyon. The shift from shade to gentle morning sunlight to harsh midday sun, then back towards those purplish hues I remembered from my first trip.

The following day we cycled further along the rim to get some perspective on the canyon. We rode through a stand of tiny conifers bonsai-ed by the wind. We saw mule deer that looked, to my Australian eyes, like inelegant moose. Best of all, we saw a Californian condor. Back in 1987 the Californian condor was declared extinct in the wild. The twenty-three that remained were caught and encouraged to breed in captivity. In 1992 scientists began to release them back into the wild and there are now more Californian condors living in the wild than in captivity—though with a population of around 440 they remain one of the rarest birds on the planet.

By the time we left the canyon, four nights after we arrived, we'd been there long enough to get down into it, travel around it and see it in every kind of light. We were sated. We certainly had no expectations of our final morning. Then at dawn, as we packed the car, half-asleep, Virginia gestured at the canyon: 'Look at that.'

I looked. What I saw was a great ocean of dense white cloud that pulsed and shimmied below the canyon's rim. It throbbed as the rising sun played across it. Day broke in a series of pale greys and blues then pink with golden flashes. The tips of the peaks scattered through the canyon floated like tiny islands. Later I learned that what we had seen was a cloud inversion. It was rare—though probably not in the same league as a Californian condor.

We stood just outside the lodge for some time. There were dozens of us lined along the rim, standing in silence, with the exception of a woman I heard muttering that the clouds were ruining the view. (Would she ask for her money back?) There is a word to describe this sense of giving over to some greater force. Numinous. Some use the word to mean religious ecstasy but for me that was not quite it, though the feeling was a reminder of why we seek nature out and what we are losing as the wilderness is driven into increasingly remote pockets of the earth.

In 2016 a female polar bear was shot in the northwest of Iceland. There have only been a few hundred recorded sightings of polar bears in Iceland. Earlier encounters, from the time before history was put into written words, have passed into folklore. It's assumed this particular polar bear had floated across on ice from Greenland. The national policy is to kill bears on sight, despite the fact they're an endangered species, on the grounds—no doubt accurate—that they tend to be hungry and dangerous after such a hazardous voyage. The version of the story I heard was that that the bear was shot while still on her ice-float but I'm sure there are other versions. Whatever the truth of the matter, the polar bear, one of only about twenty-five thousand left in the wild, is now dead. Jón Gunnar Ottósson, CEO of Iceland's Institute of Natural History, was impatient at suggestions she could have been safely moved elsewhere. 'These are dangerous animals, not some cute teddy bear,' he said. After she was shot she was, to quote the BBC, to be 'stuffed and displayed in a museum'. My point? Well, it's more an observation, really. Humans live in perilous times but things are much, much worse if you're a polar bear.

I visited Iceland in 2017. More gloaming. More tourists. That year some two million of us were expected—six times the number of people who actually live there. Friends warned me that it would be a difficult place to find a #treeoftheday. This was ironic (though perhaps only to me) since I was in Iceland to give a paper on river red gums. When the island was settled almost 1150 years ago, birch forest and woodland covered twenty-five to forty per cent of it but only the birch survived the Vikings and their axes in reasonable numbers. Grazing led to many more trees disappearing over the next three centuries.

Regular volcanic eruptions and relentless winds whip the soil away. Despite the planting of three million trees in recent years, the area of forest—estimated at about one per cent at the turn of the twentieth century—has barely increased.

I did find some very lovely old squat, downy birches and a few tough little cypresses. I asked Virginia to stand next to them, for scale, and took photos.

Iceland, like all of us, will be severely impacted by climate change in the years to come. Indeed, they might fare worse than most if the warm currents of the Gulf Stream flip, as some scientists have predicted, and plunge the country back into another ice age. Pepijn Bakker, a climate scientist at the University of Bremen in Germany, has been working on the figures.[1] If carbon emissions decrease after the year 2040 the collapse of the Gulf Stream is unlikely. If they keep rising over the next century there is a forty-four per cent chance the Gulf Stream will collapse entirely by 2300.

When William Morris rode around the country on a horse in 1871, near the seashore he came across a huge waste of black sand all powdered over with flowers, 'tufts of sea-pink and bladder-campion at regular intervals, like a Persian carpet'.[2] He asked himself, *Why do we long to send forth through the length and breadth of a land, / Dreadful with grinding of ice, and record of scarce hidden fire?*[3] I didn't see fields of flowers but did see expanses of woolly fringe moss. The moss takes

---

1   'Greenland Ice Melt Could Push Atlantic Circulation to Collapse', Rebecca Boyle, *Hakai Magazine*, January 3, 2017.

2   'Icelandic Journals', William Morris, *Collected Works of William Morris*, vol. 8, 1911.

3   'Iceland First Seen', William Morris.

centuries to grow and hugs the coal black flow of the lava fields. It's impossibly inviting. Travellers walk on it and lie on top of it as one might a doona. These passionate attentions are killing the moss and the government is scrambling to manage the footprints, literal and otherwise, left by all these visitors.

I assume Morris ate fermented shark, as I did, and found it similarly disgusting: the explosion of ammonia in the mouth, threatening to choke you, before you throw the schnapps down. But an experience Morris and I couldn't have shared was visiting the Glacier Lagoon in South Iceland. It has formed as the Breiðamerkurjökull and Vatnajökull glaciers melted over recent decades. The Icelandic government's Committee on Climate Change has warned that if melting continues at its current rate, Iceland's glaciers will be gone by the end of the next century.[4]

When we visited the lagoon at 11 p.m., small icebergs of blue ice, clear ice and sometimes dirty-snow-covered ice drifted past the shore. The bluer the ice, the more oxygenated it is. Eider ducks swam around cheerfully. Arctic terns soared and swooped through the light night sky. On another night we stood on a black beach under a heavy grey sky, in the strange glow of late evening. The light in South Iceland did something to my brain. The space between conscious and unconscious thoughts blurred. Looking into a tunnel of grey cloud settled over a glacier had a similar effect. Background loomed into foreground, volcanos lifted into the clouds and the flash of ice blue in the centre of that strange glowing light looked like an

---

4   glacierguides.is

eye. I'm not a formally religious person but I did wonder, for a moment, if looking into that landscape was like looking into the eye of God.

This collapsing of visual boundaries seemed to coincide with my general collapse into anxiety and indecisiveness. Things weren't making sense. I wondered if this was a physiological effect, the darkness of stormy weather competing with the endless day to create this impossible, counter-intuitive light. During painting classes I'd been encouraged to make background colours recessive and cooler to suggest perspective but the sky that roiled above me was neither recessive nor cool: it throbbed, alive with a glow that was not quite an aurora but was otherworldly nonetheless. As for the wind, it swept down and off the glaciers, no trees to break its fall. One morning as we drove, a gust slipped under the four-wheel drive we'd hired and lifted it slightly before dropping us gently back onto the road. A warning.

I wanted to see a puffin. I'd seen only one on the trip and that one had been dead, its beak and feet connected by a few bones and entrails lying in a puffin-like shape. Towards the end of our trip we stood on Reynisfjara beach, surrounded by signs warning of rogue waves and columns of lava that formed cathedral-like domes, buttresses, struts. It was about 10 p.m. and hundreds of us were milling about. A man stared at the control panel of his drone, which he was trying to navigate through the wind gusts up the side of the cliff. In the hope, I suppose, of filming a puffin.

We moved on from there to the next peninsula, Dyrhólaey, which was joined to the land by a spit no wider than the road we were on. The winds, expected to reach gale force by morning, were starting to pick up and I could feel them hit the side of the car, buffeting us, threatening to push us into the sea. When we got to Dyrhólaey the gates on the point were closed. No puffins for me. The disappointment turned suddenly into a deep shame. Why did I need to look at these rotund, self-contained little birds with their big flappy feet? Why couldn't I, can't we, leave them alone? I imagined the puffin looking down at us from high up on the cliffs where they roosted. Humans blundering around, ridiculous, on the sand below.

For me 2017 was a year in which physical changes, private anxieties and global catastrophes collided in a way that felt paralysing: hot flushes, sleeplessness, plummeting confidence, Trump, Brexit, a dying Barrier Reef, bombs and cars being driven into crowds, earthquakes, hurricanes and eruptions. #MeToo and the Australian equal-marriage debate just made a toxic year worse. The recurring threat on *Game of Thrones* (filmed right here! In Iceland!) was that winter was coming. And we talk about climate change like that. It's coming. But it was there in Iceland that I understood, deep in my bones, that it's not coming, it's here. The unravelling. It's begun.

No trees. Black sand. Wind. A melting glacier on the horizon covering a smouldering volcano. Our plundered planet could, if it chose, shrug us humans off with not much more than a twitch. A dull green-grey glowing sky. Such extraordinary, such incalculable beauty.

EUCALYPTUS

Sheoak *→

Dandenong ↘

* Not to scale

Rosella *

Flinders St ↓

Tawny →

Yarra

Red River gum ←

Wombat

Echidna

EUCALYPTUS

Tree e working with your body, my body,
E working with us.
While you sleep e working.
Daylight, when you walking around, e work too.

BILL NEIDJIE

W HAT did the white men of the *Endeavour* see when they
arrived on Australia's east coast? Hills covered 'with
large trees and very thick, growing to a great height
before they branch off…the leaves of one are long
and narrow, and the seed (of which I got a few) is in
the shape of a button and has a very agreeable smell.'[1]

1   Tobias Furneaux quoted in *Gum*, Ashley Hay, Duffy & Snellgrove, 2002, p. 21.

Eucalyptus are often called gum trees but not all gums are *Eucalyptus*. They refuse easy categorisation, resist answers. There are more than seven hundred species of eucalypts and endless variations. The process of naming them has taken centuries and remains incomplete. Twenty-five years ago more than a hundred trees we thought of as the genus *Eucalyptus* were recategorised as *Corymbia* or *Angophora*. As Ashley Hay documented in her wonderful book *Gum*, the time it has taken to come up with forms of classification that the taxonomists are happy with was not helped by the enthusiasm with which Joseph Banks—one of the *Endeavour*'s passengers—collected thirty thousand botanical samples then left them to sit in a drawer until he died fifty years later. Colonial Australians did not have the authority to name trees without reference to the mother country, and the mother country relied on Banks' neglected collection. Catch-22.

Eucalyptus are largely native to Australia, though some are found in Indonesia and Papua New Guinea and one species is native to the Philippines. These days, thanks to enthusiastic marketing, they're found all over the world—but they are only a handful of the more than 388 different species of tree managed by the City of Melbourne.

What trees should be planted in our streets? Since the 1970s an increasing number of Melbourne's home gardeners have been planting trees native to their area but councils are not necessarily following suit. Lorikeets, reaping the rewards of changing trends, have reappeared in Melbourne after decades of absence but the opportunity to replant Swanston

Street Walk with native trees was rejected by the Melbourne City Council as recently as 1992.[2]

There is no disputing that there is a lot to take into account when street trees are chosen. Do their roots cause damage? Do the birds and mammals they attract cause damage? Do their limbs drop on unsuspecting passers by (river red gum are notorious for such behaviour)? Will they cause problems with power lines? There are also heritage issues, which can raise even tricker questions. If a tree's job is to evoke history, whose history should it be representing? What heritage is being preserved when we plant, say, a London plane tree?

The most commonly planted trees include iconic elms (*Ulmus procera, Ulmus* × *hollandica*), plane trees (*Platanus* × *acerifolia*), river red gums (*Eucalyptus camaldulensis*), *Melaleucas*, lemon-scented gums (*Corymbia citriodora*), spotted gums (*Corymbia maculata*) and significant stands of conifers. The slender-needled *Casuarina* known as sheoak has also found some favour. Plane trees make up most of the trees within our central city, despite the fact that a sizeable percentage of the population suffer distressing asthma and coughing fits triggered by the trichome fibres planes drop in October to December. We also have particularly significant avenues of elms that survived Dutch elm disease after it laid waste to the elms of the northern hemisphere. Whatever your view on our oaks, elms and planes there is no doubt that when such trees flourish they provide wonderful shade.

---

2   Much of the information on the history of street trees in Melbourne is by Andrew May, and can be found online, at the Encyclopedia of Melbourne.

If we wanted to hark back to pre-white settlement Melbourne we'd be planting river red gums, yellow box and sheoak. In 1835, at the time of white settlement, Melbourne was a watery place alternating wetland with open forests. At the time, more than 180 bird species were counted within a two-kilometre radius of Melbourne; there were platypus in the creeks and swamps full of frogs; dingoes were common. Swamp wallabies abounded, wombats ambled here and there, emus strolled the open woodlands. Eels wound their way through the waterways and the traps local people used to catch them could still be seen in the creeks.

When the settlers arrived aggressive clearing began—so aggressive that the first peoples of the area noted a drop in rainfall caused by the loss of trees. As early as 1840, concern was voiced in the press about such rapid deforestation. While the first plantings of street trees in Melbourne didn't reverse this process, it was a start and the first significant street tree plantings were during the 1850s when Royal Parade (then Sydney Road) was planted with Tasmanian blue gums (*Eucalyptus globulus*) and radiata pine (*Pinus radiata*). Mayor Gatehouse planted the first elm tree in Collins Street next to the Melbourne Town Hall in May 1875; the city council initiated a program of systematic street tree planting three years later. Soon afterwards a letter to the editor called for higher tree guards in Carlton due to horses and cows feeding on young elms. Street trees have had a lot to contend with over the years. As well as the cows and the horses there was the issue of poor soil, inadequate drainage, infrequent watering, vandalism, gas contamination, insect infestation and disease.

By the 1930s Melbourne's eastern suburbs were characterised by avenues of the native silky oak (*Grevillea robusta*), elms and planes. St Kilda Road had all these, and added poplars into the mix. In 1936 a tree-planting campaign commemorated the coronation of George VI. Exotics—the poplar, elm, plane and oak—were favoured over native varieties.

In recent decades another significant factor in the choice of street tree has come into play: climate change. Many of the species of tree we planted a hundred years ago are struggling as they become older and Melbourne becomes hotter and drier—and it's not only introduced species that are struggling. Since the early days of settlement native trees have had their champions. The first director of Melbourne's Botanic Gardens and Victoria's first state botanist was the German-born Ferdinand von Mueller, and his passion for *Eucalyptus* inspired his life's work. He was mocked for this, and dubbed Baron Blue Gum, a nickname intended to be unkind. However the blue gum he championed, which once thrived in southeast Australia, is struggling.

In fact coastal banksia are one of the few species indigenous to Melbourne that are considered to stand a sporting chance as our climate changes. Other trees considered to have a long-term future down south include the already proven Moreton Bay figs and lemon-scented gums, as well as the less common Queensland bottle tree and bunya pine. Disease also threatens an increasing number of trees (myrtle rust and sycamore lace bug are current threats to the *Eucalyptus*, *Corymbia* and *Platanus* genera). Diversity is one way to mitigate the impact of the loss of particular species. Melbourne's Urban Forest strategy includes a commitment to plant no more than five per cent of one tree species, no more than ten per cent of one genus and no more than twenty per cent of any one family.

Whatever we plant, we need to get a move on. Within the next ten years a quarter of our current tree population will be at the end of their useful lives (including more than half of the elms) and within twenty years this figure will reach thirty-nine per cent.

We need our trees—big old trees in particular—for it is they that contribute most dramatically to the city's canopy cover. Greening the city is one of the significant ways in which a city can mitigate the extreme temperatures that are the result both of a warming climate and the fact that temperatures are often five degrees Celsius higher in our cities, creating what specialists call urban heat islands. We all know what this is like—we have driven to parts of the city where there are no trees, just baking concrete and bitumen and harsh summer sun bouncing off sheets of metal and glass. The temperatures soar above the forecast maximums and stay there. Comparable, really, to playing on centre court at the Australian Open in January.

Melbourne is not alone in this race to green itself as a

way of managing the environmental stresses ahead. Most cities struggle with maintaining, let alone increasing, their canopy as large old trees die. Singapore boasts canopy cover (depending which figures you draw on) of between 29.3 per cent[3] and 40 per cent[4] but most major cities, like Melbourne, sit at 20 per cent or even lower.

Projections indicate that by 2050 an extreme heat event in Melbourne alone could kill more than a thousand people in a few days. The City of Melbourne is trying to double its green canopy to forty per cent by 2040.[5] Wetlands are also being reintroduced, though that is to manage the city's water as well as its temperature. Increasingly there is a strategy of using 'soft' rather than 'hard' methods (like concrete drains) to absorb the water that falls and flows through the Yarra's catchment area.

Doubling our canopy is not as easy as it might sound. It's hard to plant trees at the rate needed to replace those that have died let alone to boost those numbers. Nursing young trees through the difficult early years is also tough—for it is then that they are at the greatest risk of dying and being vandalised. Too often I walk past newly planted trees to see stakes pulled out and sapling branches and trunks snapped. Even if all goes well it can take twenty years for a tree to become large enough to provide a meaningful amount of shade. If we are to meet the 2040 target most Melbourne municipal councils will have

3   'Exploring the green canopy in cities around the world', senseable.mit.edu

4   'Which is the world's most biodiverse city?', Feike De Jong, *Guardian*, July 3, 2017.

5   'Urban Forest Strategy: Making a great city greener 2012–2032', melbourne.vic.gov.au/urbanforest

to replace trees as they are lost, as well as plant new ones at a rate of approximately three thousand trees per year.[6] It's a significant investment of time and money.

The interest in a green city goes back to Melbourne's settler beginnings. In 1854 Governor La Trobe set aside 2500 acres (ten square kilometres) to create Melbourne's Royal Park. His express intent was that the land be used for recreational purposes and this included the establishment of the Brunswick Cricket Club (1858) and its early use for football (by 1865). Some land was used for grazing (which led to the trampling of native plants) as it was in other parks but, despite this, Royal Park has managed to retain stands of remnant vegetation. It is the only inner Melbourne park to do so. Some of its original wetlands have also been replaced. The Trin Warren Tamboore wetlands in the northwest corner of Royal Park were built in 2005 for storm drainage and some water purification. The treatment pond has had its banks densely planted with native plants that naturally treat the water.

Standing there in the glorious dawn, I can, for a moment, imagine what the lands we now know as Melbourne once looked like. Sheoaks shiver in the morning breeze. A ringtail possum curls up in its drey. Yellow New Holland honeyeaters flit through hedges of spiny lignum (one of the species planted for filtering purposes). There are the dark Eurasian coots with their white foreheads, dusky moorhens, purple swamphens (red bills and iridescent dark blue plumage), and so-called Pacific black ducks (brown, with stripes above and below the

---

6   melbourneurbanforestvisual.com.au

eye). Australasian grebes pull up aquatic vegetation to build a floating platform, raucous red wattlebirds call from trees, Willie wagtails flutter about for insects and welcome swallows fly a metre above the oval, hawking for insects, while rainbow lorikeets screech in the blossoms overhead.

ESCAPE TO ALCATRAZ

ESCAPE TO ALCATRAZ

I'S easy to blame the tech companies for what has been happening in San Francisco. Many of the world's largest digital corporations are based there or nearby in Silicon Valley: Google, Apple, Facebook, Twitter, Uber and Airbnb. The companies all employ a large number of people and, like most corporations, they can seem insensitive to the culture of the place where they locate their head office. The tech kids arrived looking for work a bit over a decade ago and didn't win any friends with their combination of well-paid jobs and corporate transport: buses that float through the neighbourhood early in the morning and late at night. The perception created by those blue-lit buses is similar to the fly-in, fly-out vibe of mining towns. I viewed it all with a combination of distress and fatalism that I suspect gave locals the shits: Capitalism, what're you going to do? I don't mean to suggest I was indifferent. Just that, short of a revolution, I couldn't see things changing. At least San Francisco was one of the few places in the US you could *talk* about revolution.

The strong anti-development tradition in San Francisco first emerged in the 1960s, when entire neighbourhoods were being bulldozed and freeways were carving off the edges of the city into ghettos. Being anti-development was a good thing then, but these days it's more problematic—there is such a high level of demand for places to live, not only from the rich but also the middle class and the poor, that resisting all development is no longer an option. Nimbyism is big in San Francisco. It's big back in my home town too, so I know it when I see it.

One result of all this contest and contradiction is that living in San Francisco felt, on the one hand, like living in the cradle of digital civilisation, and on the other, it felt like living *inside* Facebook. Everything fraught. So much noise. *The best lack all conviction, while the worst / Are full of passionate intensity*. (Yeats again.)

San Francisco, in short, was a city I felt ambivalent about. A city that, I'm pretty certain, felt ambivalent about me: I was a gentrifier, gauche, a woman who swore a lot, an Australian given to unintentionally smug lectures on the importance of taxation, gun control and health insurance (though never, I promise, coffee). And so I searched for a place I could escape to. There is still plenty of acid in San Francisco so I suppose I could have gone that route but the one I chose was altogether more thrilling. Gardening.

I was a gardening volunteer on Alcatraz. It's been more than two years but I'm still signed up for volunteer newsletters and get online invitations to garden in random places around the city and when I do, I want to leap on a plane, don my park services windbreaker and baseball cap and head back over. I miss the Rock (not to be confused with *The* Rock). I miss it a lot.

I learned about the possibility of volunteering there when visiting Ai Weiwei's extraordinary installations in the old laundry quarters in early 2015: massive silk dragons made out of quotes regarding the meaning of 'Freedom' and Lego portraits of men and women who have been forcibly incarcerated around the globe. That exhibition was replaced by one of photos and interviews with some of the millions of children who'd lost parents to the American incarceration industry, and that was replaced in turn with one called 'Prisoners of Age'. Some of the more striking portraits were contemporary photos of members of the Black Panthers, who'd been locked up forty years ago and *were still there*.

It's important to us, one of the rangers told me, that people don't think we're here to celebrate the prison. It's a challenge to *preserve* a colonial history without giving way to some people's desire to glorify it. While the federal prison years are a focus of tourist interest—and Alcatraz is one of the most visited National Parks in the US—site supervisor Kathyrn Daskal told me that she was keen to organise more art exhibitions, focus on the Native American occupation, and promote the gardens: to broaden an outsider's sense of the island's history and meaning. Conservation is prioritised over accessibility, which is why visitor numbers have been capped. Of course, what is to be conserved is a complicated question, too, on an island where almost everything has come from somewhere else. This includes the topsoil, much of it shipped over from nearby Angel Island carrying the seeds of the coyote brush, blue elderberry and other plants still to be found on the Rock.

Even the place itself is in part man made: Alcatraz is bigger today than it was back in 1846, but at least nowadays the soil is self-sustaining. The gardens produce abundant compost, and a rainwater catchment system was installed in 2009. Lack of water had been one of the reasons the prison was shut down in 1963. Alcatraz became a national park in June 1971 and opened to the public in 1972. During my time on the island it was the years between prison and national park that interested me most.

The island's status as a place where outsiders could make a rocky, windy home meant it was chosen as the site of a significant Native American occupation in 1969. The sit-in that ensued lasted nineteen months. In among the serious demands made by the protesters was the joke, oft repeated, that anyone who'd lived on a reservation would feel right at home on a rock that lacked basic facilities like running water. At that time Richard Oakes, a Mohawk man and one of the leaders of the action said, 'Alcatraz is not an island. It's an idea. It's the idea that you can recapture and be in control of your life and your destiny.'

During the nineteen months Oakes and the others lived on Alcatraz, ceremonies were held, connections between tribes were rebuilt; people found a way back to their heritage. It was the first occupation of its kind, triggering others that followed including Wounded Knee and the fish-ins held in waters of the Pacific Northwest. The protesters were young, which was important: these self-described Tribes of All Nations rejected the approach of their elders, one in which tribal affiliation, and a certain diffidence towards those who had stolen their land and attempted to destroy their culture, was the accepted norm.

Jane Fonda, Anthony Quinn, Buffy Sainte-Marie and Marlon Brando made shows of support by visiting the island. I like to think that's where Brando met Sacheen Littlefeather, who became famous for her poised rejection of the Oscar awarded to Brando in 1973. She spent the spring of 1971 on the island and still lives close by—across the water in Sausalito. Creedence Clearwater Revival donated fifteen thousand dollars for a boat to get people to and from the island. But the initial burst of energy dissipated over the months. Key players returned to their schools and colleges. Drug-taking escalated. Celebrity enthusiasm waned. Oakes' twelve-year-old daughter, Yvonne, died on the island after falling down some stairs. (Oakes himself died soon after the occupation was over.) In May 1971 the government turned off the electricity. In June some buildings, including the warden's house and a lighthouse, were burnt down; the argument about whether the fires were set by the government or the occupiers goes on still.

The occupation is one of the first things you are reminded of when you dock: *Peace and Freedom. Welcome. Home of the Free Indian Land.* The inscription, in bold red letters on the rebuilt water tower, is particularly eye-catching, a freshly painted replica of graffiti left during the months after the activists first commandeered the Rock. The park service spent most of 2012 and 1.5 million dollars restoring the million-litre tank and thirty-metre steel tower. The task included carefully matching the graffiti's paint and inviting the descendants of the original occupiers to participate in the work. The garden over which the water tower looms, the one around the Greenhouse, is home to poppies, roses and daisies. That's where I worked for my first few visits, toiling away under those words, looking out to the ocean at the strong currents that seemed to tear the fabric of the bay this way and that. There is also a more informal memorial, one that captures the mood of the times better than refreshed graffiti does, and you see it when you walk around to the west of the island: piles of rubble that were once homes to prison guards and now house hundreds of Pacific gulls. The houses were bulldozed after the occupation ended to make future protests harder.

Over the millennia Native Americans had come to the island to hunt sea birds but avoided living there permanently. They, like many of the more recent prisoners and guards, felt that bad spirits haunted the island. In the late 1800s, more than a dozen 'non-compliant' Hopi chiefs who wouldn't farm as the government instructed them to and opposed forced education in government boarding schools were incarcerated there. A sixteen-year-old Native American man, Clarence Carnes, was one of the men whose escape attempt triggered the Battle of Alcatraz in 1946. Carnes' parole was revoked twice, returning him to prison. He died of AIDS-related complications in 1988 and was buried in a pauper's grave. Later that same year, organised crime figure James 'Whitey' Bulgar, who had befriended Carnes while on Alcatraz, paid for his body to be exhumed and reburied on land in the Choctaw Nation of Oklahoma. This small historical detail moves me. Many snippets I hear over my time on the island move me. Nuggets small as the bullet casings that still turn up on the western side of the island. One day I found one, tangled up in the ivy that was, in turn, tangled in the *Aeonium*. Tarnished brass. Light as a feather.

We found other things as well. Bones, bits of metal, broken plates. One day an intern found a stone arrowhead that was sent off for analysis. The remains of a polystyrene totem pole sat under the piles of gum leaves that had accumulated near the docks, the remnant of the totem pole carving classes held during the occupation. Because we were dealing with archaeological finds, albeit accidentally and occasionally, we attended a lecture given by specialists on ways of dealing with these objects when we found them.

The plants themselves are archaeological relics of a kind. UC Berkeley professor Russell Beatty has described the garden's 145 species, planted by soldiers, guards and inmates over a period of more than a hundred years, as 'a significant botanical achievement', which held clues to Alcatraz's history. 'Like some of the inmates, they either made it and survived—if they were adaptable—or they didn't,' he said.[1]

Before the gardeners and the Native American acts of place-making, before it was a prison, Alcatraz was home to the seabirds. With the exception of the pelicans after which the island is named, birds have returned in their thousands. Snowy egrets, cormorants and night herons jostle for space beside the aggressive western Pacific gulls. The gulls have built nests all over the island, through the prison's ruins, and stand guard around its perimeter.

The birds, the gardens, the Native American occupation—all these seem essential to an understanding of what the Rock has become and the effect it can have on people. I volunteered over two bird-breeding seasons, which took place around each April into May. I'd walk down to the snowy egret colony. Photograph them. Sketch them. Listen to them. They are impossibly elegant birds with long trailing feathers, more delicate than any lacework, but, hilariously, they make a sound not unlike a cat vomiting up a hairball. The chicks are round and fluffy, with red feet that turn yellow

---

1 'The Plant Men of Alcatraz', Patricia Leigh Brown, *New York Times*, June 21, 2001.

as they get older. The demand for their extravagant plumes as decoration for women's hats almost drove them to extinction but the introduction of the Migratory Bird Treaty Act in 1918 helped the populations recover. (The Trump administration has issued a reinterpretation of that hundred-year-old act that substantially weakens it. 'Incidental' or 'unforeseen' harm can no longer be prosecuted: for example, the killing of a million birds as a result of the Deepwater Horizon oil spill in 2010 is no longer considered a crime.)

Snowy egrets never used to breed on Alcatraz but now they nest in bramble so thick it keeps everyone other than the odd Pacific gull (a murderous bird if ever there was one) away. When I saw them there was always a mother front and centre, and indeed when I went back through my paintings and photos I realised I'd photographed her time and time again over the fifteen or so months that I was there, without recognising she was the same bird. On my last day on the island, after the morning tea at which I was served Anzac biscuits and applauded, I went and found her a final time. She lifted her wings so they reached out to their full extent and held them up high, wing tips almost coming together. She showed me her bones, her wings, her feathers. San Francisco, sitting not far away across the water, framed her. I'm not sure if it was the constancy of my attention, the repetition of my appearance, that led to her to display herself to me in this way. Perhaps I was just lucky.

It was on Alcatraz that I met people who'd actually been born in San Francisco. Rare as hen's teeth. White retired teachers, young people who were going to college rather than working in their parents' business, an (award-winning!) organic composter who'd lived in the Mission back in the fifties, during the time it had been an Irish neighbourhood as well as a Latino one. Working the compost gang was a much sought-after position for us volunteers, but I only managed shovelling honour a couple of times. I met Bernie supporters, Hillary supporters, a solitary Trump lover, disabled adults brought to work on the island by carers. I caught the ferry once, occasionally twice, a week and watched pelicans fly past our windows in single file, saw fur seals swimming in winter, watched the muscular currents sweeping around us and wondered, for the thousandth time, did those guys really get away?

During the time I gardened there I returned to Melbourne to see Dad, and during that time I gave a talk to a group of primary school students in Clifton Hill about spending time at Alcatraz. I told them that the island sat inside San Francisco Bay. That it was a forbidding rock that rose high out of the sea, capped off by an imposing cell house and a lighthouse. That nine hectares of rock has come to mean a lot of things to a lot of people. I told them that the gardens were originally developed and tended by the military in the late 1800s. I told them about Elliott Michener, the counterfeiter-turned-gardener who planted the spectacular succulent gardens on the western side of the islands in the 1940s. He had no horticultural background but he studied books and pored over seed catalogues that guards gave him. Michener ended up working in the home and gardens of the warden, Edwin Swope. Mrs Swope, also a keen gardener, used to lay bets on horse races on Michener's behalf. When he was transferred to Leavenworth he was not happy. 'I believe that my best and only practical course is to get back to Alcatraz [where] I could at least grow Bell roses and delphiniums seven days a week and enjoy considerable freedom and trust, and in general make the best of things.'

One day I shuffled slowly down the steep western slope, in the cold bright autumn sun, helping replant the 'Persian Carpet'. First planted in the 1920s, the carpet is formed from ice plants (*Drosanthemum floribundum*) matted together. It was these plants that first enticed Michener as he was retrieving softballs outside the recreation-yard fence. He requested permission to start tending the ice plants the balls landed on, and transformed the hillside into a wall of flowers that helped hold back erosion while blooming pink and purple for several months of the year. They're known as survivor plants.

'Survivor' means all kinds of things, but in the context of the gardens at Alcatraz it's a reference to the two hundred or so plant species on the island that grew through the forty-year hiatus in care between the closure of the prison in 1963 and the arrival of the gardeners. A ninety-year-old fuchsia down by the Sally Port is one such survivor. The Persian Carpet another. Being a survivor outside Alcatraz has less cachet, and elsewhere the ice plant has been rebranded as 'invasive', which means that work gangs rip it out by the handful along coast roads. The plant was originally brought in from South Africa in the early 1900s. It stabilised the soil, but it pushed native plants out.

On Alcatraz, though, every plant was both an invader and a survivor.

I never talked to the schoolkids about the reputed hauntings, though they would have enjoyed a ghost story or two. No tourist, child or adult, comes out of the hole—a pitch-black soundproof cell where troublesome prisoners were kept for up to nineteen days—without a look of horror on their faces. But for the most part things were pretty jolly on the Rock when I was out there. One of the rangers had an impressive voice. She greeted tourists by singing Alcatraz facts to the tune of Adele's 'Rolling in the Deep'. A couple of times a week, a former prisoner called Bill Baker spruiked his memoir. He's in his eighties now and spent more than half his life in prison, four years of it in Alcatraz, and had done, he told us 'some bad things'. He got married during the time I worked there, in the particularly beautiful garden known as Officers' Row. Eloy Martinez, a member of the occupying Tribe of All Nations who once lived in a cell overlooking the island's dock with his wife and small son, now comes across from Oakland from time to time to give a tour of occupation sites across the island.

The students I spoke to had already got wind of the story of the escape attempt of 1962, during which Frank Morris and the Anglin brothers left papier-mache heads on the pillows of their beds, squeezed into ventilation ducts through openings they'd dug with modified spoons and slipped off the island on a raft made of raincoats, never to be seen again—unless you count the fictional versions of them in *Escape from Alcatraz*.

My audience listened patiently as I went on about geography and gardening, then their teacher told them they could ask questions. One little boy politely raised his hand.

'How do you make a papier-mache head?' he asked.

'Balloons,' I told him. 'Fill them up with air and slather them with newspaper and glue. Use hair swept off the floor of your local barber.'

A few weeks later I passed the message back to these miniature escape enthusiasts that one of the gardeners had taken a video of a great white shark not far from the landing dock on a day I wasn't on duty. The shark leapt out and grabbed a seal just as all the tourists were boarding the ferry. There was a lot of blood. 'Believe me,' I said to the kids, 'those guys did not get away.' I didn't manage to crush their dreams, though. After my talk they drew treasure maps and researched a variety of escape possibilities. Their teacher sent me pictures in case they might come in handy.

One and a half million visitors head out to Alcatraz each year keen to hear about the gun battles, the escape attempts (thirty-six prisoners in fourteen attempts; twenty-three caught alive, six killed, two drowned and five, including Morris and the Anglin brothers, listed as missing presumed drowned). Stories about Al Capone and the Birdman of Alcatraz are also standard fare. And in case you didn't already know this, I have to break it to you: the Birdman was no Burt Lancaster. He was an extremely violent man who knew a lot about canaries, though he wasn't allowed to keep the birds when he was held at Alcatraz.

I worked on the island through 2015 into 2016. The work on salvaging the gardens began back in 2003. Trees and flowers are still found under ivy so thick that it literally holds up fences and buildings, so old that its stems are the size of tree trunks. One cold, sunny day I was on the rocky banks on the east side, attempting to pull out ivy that hadn't been touched since 1963, before I realised that if I succeeded in getting rid of it all, I'd have nothing to stand on. Some of the banks of the island are unpredictable, not solid rock but piles of the rubble of former buildings. This is how, I realise, you end up with ruins being discovered metres below street level.

We planted survivor irises—long, gnarled rhizomes more than forty years old—in soil hardened by the long Californian drought. In truth, though, it's always been dry out there and the gardens had always been planted with species tough enough to cope without water. In the 1930s, after the island was handed over to the federal government by the military, the warden's secretary, Fred Reichel, asked the California Horticultural Society to suggest seedlings that might do well on the island. Many of the species that he imported came from the Mediterranean and were among those that flourished through the years of neglect. As well, fifteen rose species survived, including the French Bardou Job, a Welsh rose that hadn't been seen in Wales for more than a hundred years. There are gnarly old figs. There are agave that stand four metres tall and artichokes that flower violent purple, heavy with pollen, bees and humming birds. The humming birds zip and buzz in a series of straight lines, up down, left right.

One day a tiny brown one, I suppose it could be described as plain, pivoted in such a manner as to display its throat and reveal a streak of fuchsia pink of startling intensity. Perfect. And then it was gone.

When he was in his eighties Elliot Michener wrote: 'The hillside provided a refuge from the disturbances of the prison, the work a release; and it became an obsession. This one thing I would do well.' When I worked it I thought of the western side of the island as Michener's side. The windier side. The side where the succulents grow. I found that side more beautiful, by which I mean wilder. Over time some of the women I worked with came to refer to one particularly steep slope as 'Sophie's Slope' and I'm hard pressed to think of an accolade that's made me happier. I removed the oxalis that grew over and strangled the aloe vera, lying on my stomach at an angle of forty-five degrees, trying to maintain purchase without destroying the plants. It was spiky work from which I'd return home covered in scrapes and cuts. The slope looked much better over the months I worked on it but my friend Janice kept reminding me that the oxalis would just come back and she was right, it always did.

But there was something about freeing the spiky invasive plants, avoiding the aggressive Pacific gulls who were nesting, listening to the clank of the buoys, the occasional grunts of the seals, the sound of the fog horns, that filled me with joy. If I paused in my task I could sit and watch the fog snake under the bridge and across the bay; the container ships cut a swathe through the water. And I knew, because I'd seen them when standing on the mainland, that whales were feeding on schools of anchovies.

When I'd had enough of that job I'd move around to one of Michener's succulent gardens, where ninety-year-old *Aeonium* had raised the land a metre in the decades since they were planted. I pulled on ivy, following it to its source. Attempting to destroy it but knowing, in my heart, that there was no beating it, and that wasn't the point. And after each visit, as I headed for the ferry, I'd pat my fellow Australian, the survivor tea tree that scraped its arthritic long fingers along the ground.

MORETON BAY FIG

MORETON BAY FIG

(*Ficus macrophylla*)

There is no such thing as a forest. There are individual trees,
individual animals, individual birds…Trees have entitlements
too much in mind, without the obligations. There's no such
thing as entitlement, unless a tree has first met an obligation
to grow roots modestly, to drop bark and leaves discreetly,
to provide shade but not block sunlight, and never to drop its
limbs upon property owned by other individuals.

MARGARET THATCHER (kind of)

THE Meeting Tree is a massive 150-year-old Moreton Bay
fig in the Carlton Gardens. It is one of the most beautiful
in Melbourne, and has long been a meeting and gathering
place for Aboriginal people still living in the city.

Can you see it there? That big tree? In fact there's two and that's where the Aboriginal community, both before the war and when the war was on, would come and meet…on Saturday and Sunday, and during the week, but mostly weekends, everybody would come here and sit around these Moreton Bay Fig Trees. That was our meeting place in the late [19]30s and '40s and maybe early '50s.[1]

It hosts fewer meetings now, but homeless people keep clothes in its nooks and crannies. Revellers leave beer cans. When I walk past the Meeting Tree, as I do most days, I know that I am home. I think of those who lived here millennia before my Anglo-Saxon lot lobbed on them. I think of how the city has changed since I was born here, more than fifty years ago.

At night the fig is full of large and raucous fruit bats, a welcome (to me) addition to the Melbourne scene, though they can leave damage in their wake. They started arriving in the late eighties, having been driven south by habitat clearing and rising temperatures, and because of the food offered by the residential native gardens Melburnians were establishing. There was a campaign, one that drew out for years, to discourage them from using the Botanic Gardens. That story had a happy ending and the roosts relocated to a now successful colony of some fifty thousand bats at Yarra Bend Park.

<hr/>

1   'Remembering Aboriginal Fitzroy', Alick Jackomos, quoted in aboriginalhistoryofyarra.com.au

Before the bats relocated, the sky above my house went dark with them. By contrast the few that fly over our house and head for the Meeting Tree number in the tens. I'm not sure if that's because of the move or heat stress, but there is no doubt that tens of thousands die each summer when temperatures spike. Flying foxes are experiencing the greatest mammalian mass deaths in the world. The dying and dead bats fall from the trees and lie in piles below them. Possums fall as well, though in smaller numbers. Ringtail possums suffer the worst, it seems. Birds spread their wings and take to the air to cool down but they too can come crashing to the baking earth. Some days I choose not to think about these things. Instead I appreciate the hard edges of the fruit bats' wings silhouetted against the sky, their naughty, pointy faces. I walk under the Meeting Tree soon after dusk for the joy of ducking as the bats come in to land, swooping under the tree boughs, dragging them down, shrieking as they battle to find a spot to hang.

I thought of the Meeting Tree every time I met the Moreton Bay fig in the Mission, a tree that I visited from time to time: two Australian expats shooting the breeze. Moreton Bay figs are native to eastern Australia but you find them throughout California. The tallest one in California is found in San Diego. The widest is found in Santa Barbara and was planted in 1876, reportedly by a young girl who was given a seedling by an Australian sailor. The Moreton Bay fig I hung out with in the Mission was a hundred years old and lived on Cesar Chavez Street, next to St Luke's Hospital. It was one of the oldest in

San Francisco and one of only twenty 'significant' landmark trees in the city.

> Landmark trees are trees that have been designated by the Board of Supervisors as 'extra special'. It may be due to the rareness of the species, their size or age, or extraordinary structure, or ecological contribution. In addition, historical or cultural importance can qualify a tree for Landmark Status.[2]

The fig was planted next to what was once a library but is now a hospital. Protected by its designation as a landmark tree, it looks after itself first, forgets its obligations, and sheds the occasional limb onto the occasional car. Cesar Chavez, after whom the street the fig lives on was named, was more civic-minded. He co-founded the United Farm Workers union, and radicalised and supported many Latino workers in the 1960s and 1970s. His work continues to be celebrated and his portrait still adorns many of the area's murals; a parade is held in his honour each year.

The heritage Moreton Bay fig is an outlier in the district as most of the trees planted through the Mission are known as ficus (a genus that includes the Moreton Bay). *Ficus microcarpa* were originally distributed throughout Asia and into some Australian islands. Their range has extended and now includes 24th Street between Potrero and Mission. They're pale skinned with vivid small green leaves, multi-limbed, fractal; they make

---

2   www.sfdpw.org/significant-and-landmark-trees

the street distinctive. I realised that these trees were a source of contention when I was volunteering for an organisation that has its shopfront on 24th, the muralists Precita Eyes. The founder, Susan Cervantes, was agitated because a shopkeeper over the road was removing the ficus in front of their shop. The issue was, as it usually is, money. In the early 2000s the city introduced a street-tree policy that makes adjacent property owners responsible for maintaining the street trees as well as the sidewalk—whether or not the owners planted the tree, whether or not they want the tree, and whether or not they have the financial resources to care for the tree.

The *Ficus microcarpa* were planted before this law was introduced, back in the 1980s. 'They're great canopy trees,' said Doug Wildman, program director of Friends of the Urban Forest, 'and they're evergreens, so their leaves act as sponges, absorbing water and delaying a ton of storm water from running off into drains and causing floods. They were the "ideal" tree of the day.'

The eighties are over, the trees are almost forty years old and their roots cause sidewalk damage. Many of them are dying of a fungal disease caused by root pruning undertaken to try to stop that damage. *Ficus microcarpa* are no longer tree of the day.

The Mission is the oldest settlement in San Francisco. It grew up around Mission Dolores, built in 1776, one of a chain of missions the Spanish established along the west coast. The location was chosen, on the principle of taking your business to the customer, because it was close to a Native American village. I used to like visiting Mission Dolores because scenes from Alfred Hitchcock's *Vertigo* were filmed there. I also admired its fat Canary Island date palms. But the romantic appeal of the place evaporated for me once I learned that it had been a killing field. *Dolores*, the Spanish word for sorrows, proved apt by the end of 1800: there were only forty-seven Yelamu people left living there, and an estimated five thousand people buried in the cemetery and surrounding lands. At the time, the Mission's baptismal book did its best to strike a triumphant tone:

> On this day of the Feast of Corpus Christi, 1800, the conversions of heathens on this side of the bay is concluded (for the greater honor and glory of God), as today the last one was baptized…

When Americans took over from the Spanish in 1848 there were two Yelamu left, an old man and his son. Their last descendants died in the 1920s.[3]

In the days when Mission Dolores was doing its 'good' work, much of the Mission district was an interconnection of creeks (now running underground) and wetlands (now filled in) interspersed with sand dunes. There were not many trees. In *The Trees of San Francisco* Mike Sullivan says the Spanish described the area as 'the very worst place [for settlement] in

---

3   *Cool Gray City of Love: 49 Views of San Francisco*, Gary Kamiya, Bloomsbury USA, 2013.

California…since the peninsula afforded neither timber, wood nor water, nothing but sand, brambles and raging winds.'[4] Occasionally the original landscape asserts its presence. During the earthquake of 1906 soil liquefied, Mission Creek rose up, Lake Dolores re-emerged, and in one hotel alone—on the corner of Valencia and 18th—forty people drowned. I understand that the cause was liquefaction, a process common when developments have been built on reclaimed wetland; but still, it's hard not to see the old creek's rising up to swallow the building and the settlers as a form of revenge.

---

4   *The Trees of San Francisco*, Mike Sullivan, Wilderness Press, 2013.

I DON'T BLAME THE TREES

I DON'T BLAME THE TREES

YOU can see Angel Island from the east side of Alcatraz. There is only five kilometres distance between the two islands, though the currents that separate them can be fierce. Like Alcatraz, Angel Island has a complex history. The Spanish first pulled up there in 1775. Soon afterwards the Miwok people, who'd fished and hunted there for two thousand years, were driven into Mission Dolores or left the area. In 1808 Russian sea otter hunting expeditions set up a storehouse on the island. In the 1830s it was used for cattle. The army used it as a base after 1863. In 1892 a quarantine station was built, and that station was used into the 1950s.

When I first walked there I was struck by how familiar the architecture felt, as did the isolation of its beach coves. The presence of eucalypts, their fragrance, added to my sense that I knew this place. These trees do that: insinuate themselves into your very being. As I walked, I remembered, or re-remembered, that in 1968 my mother, brother and I were in quarantine at North Head, Sydney, after a trip to the United States ended unexpectedly with my parents' separation. My brother, then a baby, had not yet been vaccinated against smallpox and we were among many to be caught in the gap between the new global world of plane travel and a hidebound bureaucracy. The increase in air travel had led to heightened vigilance regarding vaccination status, and the largest number of detentions from 1951–83 were to do with whether travellers had been vaccinated against smallpox. We were among eighty-three similarly placed.[1] It was a distressing and difficult time for my mother, one made worse by our detention. My first father, Peter, once told me that there was outrage that we were detained; that our name (then Nicholls) was mentioned in the Senate. I'm too aware of the grim irony in this scenario: public

---

1   'Quarantine Station North Head 1900–1984: A history of place', Carmel Patricia Kelleher MA. PhD thesis, Department of Modern History, Politics and International Relations, Macquarie University, May 2014.

outrage that we, a white Australian family of three, might have been forcibly held in detention for two weeks.

People had been detained at North Head over a period of 150 years. Smallpox, typhoid, influenza and plague outbreaks were sometimes the reason for this, though detainees also included migrants from what we now call the UK, from China, Indochina, Vietnam and Timor. At times evacuees from disasters such as Cyclone Tracy found themselves living in the station.

Memories of that time flicker occasionally, like decomposing photographs or old sound recordings. I see rabbits dash across lawns at night, I hear a nurse earnestly telling me to eat carrots, like the rabbits did, so I could see better when I peered into the darkness. I can smell, I can hear, the ocean. I seem to remember making sandcastles on a tiny beach cove while a nurse looked on in her starched uniform, though I wonder now how I could have remembered the starch. It seems to be far too writerly a detail for a four-year-old to focus on. Perhaps most of what I remember of that time is simply some kind of bolstering, a starching, of the truth. I went on a tour to visit the centre not so long ago, though eschewed the ghost tour. As I walked through the old buildings, I remembered living in one of the weatherboard and corrugated-iron huts; being bathed in the hospital-green bathtubs. Again, I suspect that was my imagination working overtime.

The dormitories on Angel Island are desolate. Run down. During San Francisco's foggy, windy summers they would have been damp and cold. Nonetheless, they can stand comparison with Sydney's quarantine station, which has received the kind of rebranding that seeks to erase the past. The station on Angel Island feels like what it once was: an immigration camp. Chinese immigrants arriving during the gold rush of 1848 encountered hostility, particularly from the unions. The Chinese Exclusion Act was passed in 1882 to deny them citizenship, and this exclusionary state of affairs continued, in various ways, until 1940. From 1910–40 Chinese immigrants were held on Angel Island for months, sometimes years. Over that time they were interrogated in the hope that they would trip up in their stories somehow and thus could be deported home. When you walk around the dorms you see Chinese characters carved into the walls, the remains of some two hundred poems. The paint and putty the guards used to cover up the poetry simply highlight the dints and draw attention to the fact that these walls can talk. As an article in the *New York Times* noted:

> The formal qualities of the poetry—which was written, for the most part, by men and women who had no more than an elementary education—tend to get lost in English translation, but its emotional force comes through. One poem reads, 'With a hundred kinds of oppressive laws, they mistreat us Chinese. / It is still not enough after being interrogated and

investigated several times; / We also have to have our chests examined while naked.'[2]

During World War II, Japanese Americans were interned there, among other places. Many of them had lived in America for more generations than their white neighbours. Take Makoto Hagiwara, a Japanese immigrant and gardener, who was the official caretaker of the Japanese Tea Garden at Golden Gate Park from 1895 until his death in 1925. He pruned trees and shrubs into the shape of clouds and birds, and the tea gardens he looked after were the oldest in the country. After he died his daughter, Takano Hagiwara, and her children became the proprietors of the garden, which they in turn worked, until the US declared war on Japan and moved the family to an internment camp. At the war's end they were neither allowed back nor offered reimbursement. The garden itself suffered and many rare plants were left to die.

The fierce debate about whether to remove the eucalypts from Angel Island, and the best way to do so, went on for some years towards the end of the twentieth century. The debate was (still is) loaded with words and phrases like 'native', 'refugee', 'immigrant', 'invader', and phrases like 'ethnic cleansing'[3]— even though, as the San Diego County's chief entomologist in the 1990s pointed out—California's humans were 'not natives either'. After a battle that lasted six years it was agreed that eighty out of eighty-six acres of eucalypts were to be removed

2 'The Lost Poetry of the Angel Island Detention Center,' Beenish Ahmed, *New Yorker*, February 22, 2017.

3 *Trees in Paradise*, Jared Farmer, W. W. Norton, 2013.

and herbicides used on the tree stumps. One of the reasons the debate about eucalypts had become so contentious was the concern that the trees contributed to wildfire. It was argued that averting fire was worth the risk of environmental damage caused by poison. It made no difference in this case and in 2008, ten years after the removal of the eucalypts, almost half of Angel Island was engulfed by a massive brush fire that burned so brightly it could be seen from miles, from counties, away.

Did it matter if those trees, more than a century old, died? They were not, after all, from that place. It's a hard question to consider when almost all of us now—flora, fauna and humans—are from somewhere else.

In the early 1900s the graves of San Francisco were opened, the remains exhumed and relocated to the south of the city. In May 2016 a casket that had been missed was found under a garage floor. In it was the body of a young girl.

> Nobody knows her name or how she died. She lay under a San Francisco home's concrete garage floor for decades until two weeks ago, when workers doing remodelling struck her lead-and-bronze coffin with their shovels…She looks, through the two glass windows of the coffin, like a young girl and not like the 145-year-old remains of one…Lying beside her are eucalyptus leaves.[4]

------

4   'Little girl, rose still in hand, found in coffin beneath SF home', Steve Rubenstein, *San Francisco Chronicle*, May 25, 2016.

The owner of the premises on which the coffin was found was told that the body was on her private property, and thus owned by her. Furthermore the owner was not allowed to rebury the coffin, as she didn't have a death certificate. The owner, who marketed cookies for a living and did not have the money to maintain the girl-now-artefact, stated: 'I understand if a tree is on your property, that's your responsibility. But this is different. The city decided to move all these bodies 100 years ago, and they should stand behind their decision.'

These days eucalypts define San Francisco's landscape much as the palm defines Los Angeles. The writer Jack London planted a hundred thousand Tasmanian blue gums (*E. globulus*) on his estate at the beginning of the twentieth century in the hope of cashing in on the increased demand for lumber after the San Francisco earthquake of 1906. That estate is now a state park. It boasts oak woodlands, as well as stands of the blue gums that survived his enraged culling when it transpired that, 'despite his careful research with scientists at University of California in Davis and diligent plans', the crops were not usable for building, for paper, or 'for much of anything'.[5] A fact, of sorts, that had been established some thirty years earlier.

Jack London was not the only one to experience enthusiasm then regret. Overblown claims combined with ignorance of how best to prepare the wood for lumber meant that the eucalyptus bubble first burst in the 1880s, then slowly expanded again before finally popping for good in 1916.

---

5   http://jacklondonpark.com

The Californian gold rush, with its demands for construction materials and fuel, had put pressure on wood supplies. Deforestation had become a serious concern. This coincided with the Golden Gate Nursery in San Francisco stocking Tasmanian blue gum seedlings—no doubt in response to the passionate advocacy of Victoria's first state botanist, Ferdinand von Mueller. His passion for *Eucalyptus* (he eventually published the ten-volume *Eucalyptographia*) was particularly focused on the blue gum (which was not, despite its name, to be found only in Tasmania). Mueller, and governments and individuals around the world who listened to him, came to believe blue gums cured malaria, which was not true (and that its oil was an antiseptic, which was). They could, however, help drain swamps, and that may have been the source of the malaria rumours. They grew quickly and were believed to be a good building material—which was also true if they were allowed to mature, but not if they were harvested after only ten or twenty years.

In a state built on a gamble, *Eucalyptus* became subject to a rush of its own. In the late 1800s millions of blue gums were planted throughout the Bay Area. Frank C. Havens, an Oakland developer, planted eight million of them in a twenty-two kilometre strip from Berkeley through Oakland. In 1868 the California Tree Culture Act was created to encourage people to replace the oak trees and redwoods that had been cut down. The modish blue gums were there to fill the breach; but it soon became apparent that they took too much water out of the soil and had been planted so as to create a monoculture that resulted in piles of shed bark and limbs.

Despite its deficiencies as a building material, the young eucalypt remained useful for windbreaks and fuel. And despite breaking the hearts of some entrepreneurs, the blue gums flourished and self-propagated to become forests—or, to use the loaded biological language of the day, went native. Better than that, according to Abbot Kinney back in 1895, California had taken a tree that was 'scrawny' in its homeland and improved it, practically creating a new genus. That was another exaggeration of course, though Kinney was right that California's eucalypts are often larger and broader than in Australia. *Eucalyptus* were at home in California and, conversely, made Californians (themselves an assortment of non-natives) feel that they were home. One or two generations of Californians thought the trees were natives. "'Say,'" an American serviceman had reportedly drawled in Sydney during World War II, "you got some of our eucalypts here.'"[6]

When I first arrived in San Francisco I saw blue gums everywhere I looked. On Alcatraz, in Golden Gate Park, in the former military complex, the Presidio, down by the Golden Gate Bridge. That was where there were a series of art installations by environmental artist Andy Goldsworthy, many of them using the blue gum. One of these installations, Wood Fall, is a path of zigzagging tree trunks that snake for hundreds of metres along one of the city's oldest footpaths, known as Lover's Lane, and is made entirely from fallen eucalypts

6   Hay, p. 151.

planted in the late nineteenth and early twentieth centuries. Goldsworthy described the work as 'drawing the place'.

I felt a certain proprietorial pride in the trees that I thought of as 'ours' or even 'mine', so it took me a while to notice the signs that some Californians had fallen out of love with the tree once thought of as a miracle. Then I read a newspaper article that described activists pressing their naked bodies against one of the tallest stands of hardwoods left in California. They were drawing attention to the fact that these trees, blue gums in the Eucalyptus Grove along Strawberry Creek on the Berkeley campus of the University of California, were slated for removal. Ageing hippies, activism, nudism. The story cheered me. It kept alive my hope that people still cared about things environmental. I applied for a fellowship to write about *Eucalyptus* asking the following questions: What is it about the eucalypt that inflames both hatred and devotion? How do we save the eucalypt from becoming the fall guy for the delusions of capitalism and the desire for expansion? What does it mean to be 'native' or 'non-native' in a global world?

The questions were either over- or underwhelming. Perhaps both. I did not get the fellowship but by that point I was too obsessed with the blue gum—it does that to people—to stop researching. I read newspapers and found stories of trees being removed from public land in the dead of night, reducing those who love them to endless days in court. I learned that in 1984, five million dollars was set aside to systematically remove 'exotic plant species capable of naturalising' to allow for the return of native flora and fauna. The US Forest Service listed eucalypts as hazardous because they shed bark and limbs (though they've also said that it's better to leave trees in place, non-native or otherwise, rather than pursue deforestation as a form of fire management).

Blue gums were of particular concern because they used a lot of water and had a high oil content (though other trees including the California bay laurel have a higher oil content). It's also fair to say that eucalypts don't support local flora and fauna in the way native trees do, though they have been around long enough to begin to ingratiate themselves with the environment. When driving down to Los Angeles from San Francisco I visited monarch butterflies in a eucalyptus grove at Pismo Beach. The sight of clusters of orange and black butterflies lifting in a golden explosion as the morning sun hit the trees' limbs was something to behold. Each year the eastern monarchs migrate thousands of kilometres from as far as Canada, down to Florida and Mexico. Their traditional habitats have been destroyed over the last century and now it is eucalypts that provide a winter home for them. Once numbered in the millions, the monarch butterfly population now sits at around twenty thousand. Pesticides, climate change and a declining eucalypt population are some of the reasons for this.

There was a moment when the eucalypt's fortunes swung from a 'Wonder-Tree, Tree of Hope, Tree of Fulfilment' (to quote Jared Farmer); to an invasive fireweed that needs to be 'exterminated', a 'gasoline tree'. That moment was the Oakland firestorm of 1991. More than three thousand city houses and hundreds of apartments were destroyed. Twenty-five people died. Eucalypts and the fuel load they created were blamed. But if *Eucalyptus* really were responsible for the 1991 Oakland firestorm, why are so many organisations still arguing about what to do with them some twenty-five years later? In 2016, 5.67 million dollars was granted to the Federal Emergency Management Agency (FEMA) for tree-cutting projects aimed at reducing the risk of wildfire. The City of Oakland, UC Berkeley and the East Bay Regional Park District were to share the funds. A number of parties—the Sierra Club, FEMA, UC Berkeley, the Hills Conservation Network and the City of Oakland—were at odds about how it should be done. The Sierra Club, which, along with the City of Oakland and UC Berkeley supported the removal of all non-native trees, and the Hills Conservation Network, a neighbourhood group that does not support the trees' removal, filed suit separately after FEMA released a final version of an environmental-impact (EI) statement. Both parties found the EI deficient, though for different reasons. This was not the first time the fate of the eucalyptus was taken to the courts. Put simply the question under debate was: what replaces trees if you remove them? And will that environment be more fire safe? Litigation has considered that question four times, and four times the outcome has gone against tree removal.

I wondered how much of this argument was a desire to avoid the fact that it costs money to manage the wildland–urban interface, money that the City of Oakland was reluctant to spend, or simply did not have? And, to get back to the blue gums of Strawberry Creek, where did UC Berkeley's plan for expansion fit in?

In an attempt to get some answers to these questions I interviewed one of the members of the Hills Conservation Network, Peter Scott. We sat in his house in the Berkeley Hills, which had been rebuilt after burning down in 1991. Peter set out his concerns about the ways in which developers were exploiting anxiety about fire. He pointed out to me that the university was looking to put up more buildings on campus and needed an excuse to remove the trees. They were less ready to focus on other fire-related issues such as empty reservoirs and the lack of standardisation among fire hydrants which led to mismatches between fire-hose attachments and fire-hydrant fittings.

I asked Peter where he was on the day of the Oakland firestorm and he told me he had been working out of town. I commented that that would be quite a relief in one way as there was little he could have done to protect his house. He hesitated then said, no, not really: his mother had been living with him and his family. She'd called his sister three times asking her to organise help and his sister, in turn, had been on the phone to the fire department. This was to no avail, in part because of the empty water tanks and the incompatible fittings on hydrants and fire trucks. The house burned and his mother died as she waited for help.

Peter went on to tell me that his daughter, who was a teenager at that time, had been so deeply traumatised by the death of her grandmother, the loss of their home and the instability of the years that followed that she eventually committed suicide.

Peter was working hard to maintain a certain reserve. 'I want to make it clear,' he said to me, 'that I don't blame the trees.'

During summer and fall, 2018, California experienced its greatest wildfires in recorded history. The worst of these, the Camp Fire, burned over six hundred square kilometres and destroyed more than eighteen thousand structures, most of them within the first four hours of the blaze. It claimed at least eighty-five lives. At the time of writing, more than two hundred people were still missing and thousands were living in tent cities. Significantly, the firestorm spread from house to house rather than from tree to tree. The pine trees of Paradise, the town most devastated by the fires, still had their canopies intact: winds pushed the fire along so fast it never rose into them. While the Camp Fire raged, a second fire system, the Woolsley, burned just south of LA. That fire destroyed 1643 structures and wildlife habitats and killed three people. Two southern mountain lions, P-74 and P-64, also died.

Fire and environmental historian Stephen Pyne speaks and writes with the passionate conviction of a man convinced we are on the brink. When I lived in San Francisco I attended a lecture he gave on the importance of allowing fire to do its part in maintaining the environment. Low-intensity fires used to burn off undergrowth and other fire fuel were the way the ecosystem maintained itself; the way that Native

Americans and Indigenous Australians used to manage their environment. In recent years American fire services have stopped doing prescribed burns because of the law and public and political anxiety on the subject. There is a tentative return to the practice in some states, including California, but prescribed burning remains underutilised.

These days tens of millions of people are living in an environment known as the wildland–urban interface. In California it is mandated that people clear thirty metres around their houses, but that requirement stops at individual property lines and homes are still built close to one another. Fire policy also needs to distinguish between structure fires and wildland fire. For reasons that include increases in both temperatures and fuel loads, fires are burning hotter and becoming more dangerous. In Australia, as with California, the fire season is—according to fire agencies in both countries—now close to continuous throughout the year.

When I discussed these issues with Peter Scott he reminded me that nearly all destructive California wildfires have been brush-and-grass fires, which move and change direction so quickly firefighters can't contain them, as had been the case on Angel Island. Trees, in contrast, provide a canopy that shades the understorey, mitigates winds, raises the moisture at ground level, discourages the growth of weedy, flammable plants, and slows the progress of fire when it does ignite. When forests do burn, old-growth forests don't do so as intensely as younger forests—but we are losing our old-growth forests.

I'm leaving the last word on this to Peter—he's had more reason than most to think about these issues. He was graceful about me using his words as the title for this essay, but not convinced. If you're going to argue that you shouldn't blame the trees, Peter said to me, you *have* to ask the question, *why not?* And the answer to that question is that trees are not the problem. Trees are the *solution*.

MEXICAN FAN PALM

MEXICAN FAN PALM

(Washingtonia robusta)

The palm stands on the edge of space.
WALLACE STEVENS

VIRGINIA and I have driven Highway One, north and south of San Francisco, dozens of times. It felt like a privilege every time because it was clear to us that sections of the road would not last much longer. As I was writing this essay, a year after my return, I was not surprised to find out that my favourite guesthouse on that highway, the eighty-year-old Deetjans, with its cedar-lined rooms untouched by locks or internet connections, its fluffy doonas and open fires, had been seriously damaged in a mudslide. Swathes of the highway were closed south of Julia Pfeiffer Burns State Park.

When we drove north of San Francisco there were often flooded sections of road that sat below sea level. We once saw a family of otters dash along a sliver of beach by the highway before disappearing into a pile of rocks, heading I know not where. Virginia swam in Tomales Bay one warm spring day, only to be shown iPhone footage of the (non-great white) shark that was swimming close by. We'd been told many times about the great white breeding ground not so far away, which meant that in my imagination Tomales Bay was just a mass of great whites leaping out of the ocean with seal pups in their mouth, 24/7. Indeed a shark had recently been filmed doing just that by the ferry launch at Alcatraz.

We'd opened fresh oysters and eaten them with a cold beer in the picnic grounds that hovered between sea and gutter. We'd wound around the coast, high up into the fog then down again, only to find, once we were below the fog line, that there was yet more fog, inverted over the Pacific Ocean, a veritable sea of cloud, catching the sun as it set in a rainbow of greys and dusky pinks, gold, violet and blue. An extraordinary sight; one I'd been lucky enough to see not once but twice in a single year.

To the south of San Francisco we'd walked under the lichen dripping from cypress at Point Lobos and watched flocks of pelicans—smaller and darker than the Australian pelican—stream through the sky. Soon after that, for more than a hundred kilometres, cliffs plunged down into beds of giant kelp that lurched in the wild ocean below. They rose up on the other side of the road also, dotted with pampas grass, or with cypress, or the signs of recent landslides. There used to be more than a million sea otters in the world, but these days there are only a hundred thousand worldwide. Three thousand of those live on this coastline. We saw them holding hands and surfing. Rafts of ratbags, their squeals rising up the cliff to greet us. Ocean spray rose high up also, though it never made it to where we stood. The views were variously windswept and clear, or taken in through the filter of cypress leaves and branches. Just the once we saw a condor circling high above Julia Pfeiffer Burns State Park. Closer to Los Angeles, near Hearst Castle, we stopped to see the elephant seals: seals giving birth, Pacific gulls pecking at the pups as soon as they slid out, bull seals rolling on the newborns as they heaved themselves up to hump the mothers exhausted from giving birth, from feeding their young, from not eating. The beach stank of shit and blood and rang with the screams of hungry pups, assaulted mothers, horny bulls and bachelor seals vying for attention by crashing their chests together in the surf. We half-cried, half-stood back in amazement at this appalling sight. One of the young girls we were travelling with, our friend Elsie, turned to her mum and said she didn't think she ever wanted a boyfriend. We tried to explain that things were different in the animal kingdom, but I don't think any of us were convinced.

On one of our trips to Los Angeles we abandoned Highway One and drove the more efficient I-5. As we were driving we saw a large semi-trailer carrying a mature palm tree. Virginia, an excellent supporter of @sophtreeofday, leaned out the window on the passenger's side and took some pictures for me. It's no easy task to transplant a mature palm. You need palm experts to tie up the fronds and excavate the root ball. It takes a crane to place the tree in its new home. The tree, having survived being uprooted from the soil where it first grew, needs to cope with being inserted into a concrete-lined street, with few fellow trees to protect it from the radiant heat. There are palms that are native to California, but most of the iconic palms that define Los Angeles streets are from Mexico. They were chosen by the Division of Forestry, looking for cheap, uniform street trees that could be planted by Depression-relief teams before the LA Olympics in 1932.

The previous Los Angeles favourite was what Australians call the peppercorn, but it, like the ficus in San Francisco, got a bad reputation for buckling sidewalks. Melbourne folk are often quite sentimental about the peppercorn, and a stand of them runs the length of the Kensington stock route down from the Kensington Newmarket Saleyards on the corner of Racecourse and Smithfield roads. The saleyards opened in 1861, the year the Melbourne Cup was first run just across the road. Drovers used to walk the animals up from the ports, and eventually the roads were built to accommodate this. At its height of activity in 1944, 6.5 million sheep went through the saleyard. My mother tells me that my grandfather, a farmer from Tylden, purchased his sheep here during the late spring and summer sales. That there was a saying that went: 'Horses never, cattle sometimes but you can always shear an income.' The peppercorns that line the bluestone lanes between the saleyards and the Maribyrnong River were planted in the 1920s. Their job was to provide shade for the hundreds and thousands of animals that were herded along here for three and a half kilometres before crossing Lynch's Bridge to the Angliss Meatworks in Footscray. As time went on the animals were herded at night because of concerns that local residents would be stampeded as they went about their daily business. I took to regularly walking that line of trees, under fronds and pink peppercorns that swayed in the breeze. Despite this bucolic scene, it wasn't hard to imagine the sheep, the cattle, sweating, frantic, as they were driven towards a fearful death.

'Older trees grow top heavy, can blow down in storms and are consequently no longer planted on public streets in Riverside, California for fear of lawsuits', I read in a Victorian environmental impact statement that set out why Victorians should avoid the peppercorn as Californians now do. It has 'potential to cause damage to property, though this appears not directly as a result of its growth habit. Its gum is also documented as causing damage to car duco.' On the plus side: 'In degraded locations mature trees may provide food and shelter to native animals including birds, bats and possums' and 'provide some assistance in food and shelter to desirable species'.

When I read that my first thought was: fuck car duco

and fuck fear of lawsuits. My second thought was that those peppercorns provided some much needed shelter to me at primary school. My third thought was that most of the planet could now be described as a degraded location.

In 1931 alone more than twenty-five thousand Mexican palm trees were planted in Los Angeles. Many of these are reaching the end of their lives. Now palms, like peppercorns, will be replaced with trees that provide more shelter and use less water. Over the few days we were in Los Angeles I tried and failed to imagine the city without them; but I assume that one day there will be pictures of the palms of Los Angeles in a museum, much as there are pictures of the oaks of Oakland in the Oakland Museum. And some person in the future will look at that photo and think how strange Los Angeles looks with boulevards lined by tall palms, all slightly inclined towards the Santa Ana winds. For balance.

IN THE LONG RUN THE HOUSE ALWAYS WINS

IN THE LONG RUN THE HOUSE ALWAYS WINS

THERE are two men I refer to as my father, or call Dad. It's a situation people find confusing so I'll walk you through it. I was born in Melbourne in 1963 to Peter Nicholls and Sari Wawn. In 1968 they travelled to the US with my brother and me; the marriage dissolved fairly quickly once we got there and Saul, Mum and I returned to Australia. Mum met John in 1969. Peter stayed overseas until the late 1980s. John adopted my brother and me. I have two birth certificates. Sophia Alice Nicholls, Sophia Alice Cunningham. There are two versions of me, and the fathers of both versions have died in the last two years.

After John, who I called Dad, was diagnosed with frontal lobe dementia, I read an article that described how long it could take the symptoms of the disease to develop and the personality transformation that went with it. At the time I felt some relief that our interactions, increasingly repetitive and uncomfortable, hadn't just been him, or me. (Whatever 'him' meant. Whatever 'I' am.)

I don't mean to imply that one day my dad was perfect, then he changed and the difficult things about him were merely symptoms. Life isn't like that either. What I'm trying to say is that in 2002 my dad came to stay in my flat in Melbourne. A neighbour and friend told me that he kept making passes at her and she hid when she heard him coming. He got worked up about cyclists using the road; he got worked up about all kinds of things. He made rude comments about the food I cooked. I started to count the number of bottles left in the recycling and was shocked. I knew Dad drank too much but seriously, I'd had no idea.

In 2003 I had a phone call from Jakarta. Dad wanted me to look at a flat he was thinking of buying. He needed me to see it in the next hour, despite the fact that I was at work, that I had meetings. I went and looked at the flat. It wasn't right.

In 2004 I had a call from Jakarta. Dad wanted me to check

out a short-term rental unit for his next trip home. I did so, and then sent him an email about its various qualities. He called me again and asked me to go and visit it at different times of day so I could let him know how much sun it got through the day. He particularly wanted to know if the morning light would be good. I said no. When he arrived to look at houses for himself, he drank heavily, wandered the house all night and left the television on with the sound dialled up to full blast.

In 2005 Dad came to town and I organised to take him out to dinner. He wanted to meet in a bar, which I then couldn't get him to leave. We finally made it to dinner, and he ordered many entrees then didn't eat a thing. Maybe this is the trip where he got upset that I wouldn't organise tickets for him to various shows? I can't remember. I do remember that he never paid me back in those days, not because he was ungenerous but because he'd forget to do so, and I could not afford to spend thousands of dollars on his account. Later I realised that he was pressuring me to organise these things for him because he no longer knew how to use the internet, but instead of understanding that, I just got really annoyed.

In 2006 Dad bought a house nine hours' drive from where I lived and left Indonesia so he could live there. He did not seem to understand the logistics of this: that I could not easily visit. I drove up one Melbourne Cup weekend and spent most of the trip looking for lost paperwork so Dad could sort out his partner's visa situation. I did a lot of cleaning.

In 2007 Dad turned sixty. He abandoned the idea of living

on the south coast of New South Wales and moved back to Bali, though sometime that year he also came to Melbourne for a visit. Probably to see the dentist. There is a dentist living in the suburbs of Melbourne who made tens of thousands of dollars out of Dad's final years. Anyway. I got a phone call. He was stuck down the side of the house he was staying in and couldn't figure out how to get inside the house. I suppose it's obvious to readers that my Dad had dementia and it crossed my mind, it's true. But he was so young. Everyone who knew him would testify to this. His youthfulness.

In 2008 Dad got married, at short notice, in Bali. My brother and I flew over for the wedding. He was overwhelmed with joy to be marrying his wife. They loved each other. Soon after the wedding he visited Melbourne to see the dentist. He called me to say there was a problem with the key to the house he was staying in, so I drove to the house, opened the front door, and took him to the pub for a drink.

In 2009 Dad stayed in an apartment four minutes' walk from my house. I was cooking dinner for him. He called to ask me to pick him up because his knees were hurting. I told him that I lived in a one-way street and that it was not easy to drive by. Half an hour later he still hadn't arrived, so I looked, then found him, lost, in the middle of the street. He'd forgotten which house was mine but he'd been talking to people along the way and made some new friends. Dad was always making new friends. I brought him home and gave him his meal but he pushed the meat around on his plate and made shapes out of the vegetables. He said he didn't like the food. He was sixty-one. Too old to be behaving like this. Too young to be behaving like this.

The next day I got a phone call from Dad. He wanted to be taken to Victoria Market to buy a shirt. We went to the market and bought a shirt.

The day after that I had a phone call from Dad. He wanted to be taken to Victoria Market to buy a shirt. We went to the market and bought a shirt.

The day after that I had a phone call from Dad. He wanted to be taken to Victoria Market to buy a shirt. We went to the market and bought a shirt. That day I stood in an aisle at Victoria Market and watched Dad exclaim with pleasure over the various shirts hanging there, and suddenly I understood. Just like that. Clear as day. Dad no longer knew how to find the shirts he'd packed, or that he'd worn once and thrown aside (in the dishwasher I later discovered) to be laundered. Dad was losing not just his shirts but his mind.

My memory is a bit hazy and it's hard to remember if we had lunch the day I understood that Dad, despite his youth, had some kind of dementia. Maybe it was the next day. Whatever. We had lunch. I planned to tell Dad that I thought there was a problem and that he needed to see a doctor. But what actually happened was that Dad took my hand and started to cry.

We saw a GP called, I kid you not, Dr Hope, and it was suggested that Dad had Alzheimer's but more tests were needed.

'I can beat this,' Dad said, then took the next plane home,

forgoing further tests. I don't blame him. Tests weren't going to change things, we all knew that.

In 2011 I was writing a book, which required me to spend time in Darwin. When I was there Dad and his wife decided to join me: it was easy to get there from Bali, and they needed access to healthcare.

One evening I took them to the sailing club to eat a meal as the sun went down. Something about the food reminded Dad of his childhood and he talked about potatoes and how his mother used to cook them. The memory pleased him. When the waitress asked him if he liked his meal, he told her they were the best potatoes he'd ever had.

The waitress was brusque: you're kidding me, right? I took her aside and asked her to back off. This was happening more and more: Dad could no longer cover up, hard as he tried, and people didn't know how to respond to him. I watched Dad perform for the doctors. He was valiant. He was given a revised diagnosis of frontal lobe dementia. Similar to Alzheimer's, but different.

'He'll live with it longer,' the doctor told me, 'and he'll know what's happening for longer than is fair.' I had to hand it to this doctor. He was a straight shooter.

It was on that same trip that I took Dad to a morning tea and trivia quiz for people with dementia. These folk might have had cognitive impairment, but they sure could remember the details of movies they'd seen decades ago. Old ladies leapt in the air, hands raised, yelling, *The China Syndrome*! *Dirty Dancing*! There were some films that didn't make their way into the quiz, I noted. I found myself thinking of one of Dad's favourites, *One Flew over the Cuckoo's Nest*. Nope. Too close to the bone. That wasn't going to get a look in.

In the last category they played snippets of songs so people could name the tune and at one point John Lennon's 'Imagine' came on. I looked for the door, desperate to get out before my sobs became too loud but it was too late. Everyone was singing along, waving their hands in the air as if they were at a concert. Dad could no longer sing along but he smiled and smiled and smiled.

Imagine.

In early 2016 I was in LA because I wanted to do some more research on *Eucalyptus* in California. Something Maggie Nelson wrote about the city stayed with me: 'The Santa Ana winds are shredding the bark off the eucalyptus trees in long white stripes.' Yes. A second reason I was there was that a mountain lion called P-22 that lived in Griffith Park had recently eaten an elderly Australian koala called Killarney. I'd written dozens of emails, to biologists, journalists, city councillors and magazines hoping to get some traction on a story about P-22. I'd only had two replies. Both negative, though one very kind, from an editor who said he liked the story but the koala was a bit too tenuous a link to an Australian audience. Discouraged, I was still keen to do what research I could in the days that I had.

Fifteen months after that trip I finally had a chance to write about P-22. It had been a long break, so I decided to paint my way back into writing. There are many photos of the lion but I used a photograph taken by the *National Geographic* photographer Steve Winter back in 2013. You may know it. P-22 strides from the left of frame to the right, down a hill, muscles rippling, eyes glowing, enormous paws padding. The Hollywood sign is above him in the middle distance. One of the things that happens when you paint with watercolour is that the water and the pigment act in ways that are suggestive. So, for example, the umber I chose for P-22's body melted into the sienna of the earth below him and the indigo of the sky above. I looked at the photo closely. Registered his enormous paws. His eyes were a dull gold, as, indeed, was his coat, though that blended into the beige and white of his underside—neck, belly, inner thighs and forelegs. In the photo he was looking directly ahead but my painting was slightly off so it made the most sense to have him looking away from me. I found that I hadn't left enough room on the paper for his enormous head. He exited the side of the page just before the tip of his nose. I didn't get his eye right, either, so my picture has him glancing back at me warily as he tries to slip away, rather than looking confidently ahead as he does in the photo. I took that as part of what the painting had to teach me. A reminder that this wild animal was shy, alert to danger. That he could disappear into the background if needed.

P-22 is the only mountain lion (also known as the cougar, or puma) to have got himself successfully from the Santa Monica Mountains to Griffith Park, at least since 2004 when scientists began tracking such things. The trek involves crossing the two busiest freeways in the United States and most of the animals who try it—mountain lions, coyotes, mule deer, bobcats, raccoons, skunks, foxes, American badgers, long-tailed weasels, ring-tailed cats—have died in the attempt, though it seems that coyotes do better than other animals. The freeways are such a barrier that the population of bobcats living east of Interstate 405 (out Pasadena way) and south of Route 101 (down towards Malibu) are genetically distinct from the bobcats of Thousand Oaks. It's possible, of course, that P-22 found a less hazardous way across. A culvert, perhaps, or one of the bridges that cross the Hollywood Freeway. (A young relative of P-22's, P-64, was known, before his recent death in the Woolsley Fire, as the Culvert Cat because of his ability to negotiate the freeways by moving through the drains underneath them.)

P-22's success made him a poster boy for Predators in the City. And there are a lot of them: leopards in Mumbai, peregrine falcons in New York and Melbourne, polar bears in Churchill, Manitoba, grizzly bears (and moose) in Anchorage, coyotes in San Francisco, pythons in Miami, great white sharks in (well, near) Perth, kangaroos throughout Canberra, crocodiles in Darwin, foxes in London and everywhere else. The stories told about these animals vary from the celebratory—only the brave and clever survive in urban environments!—to the devastating: mountain lions have been found in LA with their heads and paws cut off, grizzly bears are treated like problem children and hauled off to zoos, moose drink too much, so do some elephants, who also raid villages and kill humans before being slaughtered in return, leopards nab toddlers and as a consequence are trapped (if they're lucky) then thrown into overcrowded territories where they cannot thrive, the polar bears are starving as their world contracts around them like a vice.

The Santa Monica Mountains Fund is raising money to build a wildlife crossing at Liberty Canyon in an attempt to release the territorial pressure. Stasis is a death knell for mountain lions and other species: the inbreeding and consequent loss of genetic diversity that arise when populations are contained in too small an area are devastating. Greater susceptibility to disease; greater propensity for violence towards each other. On the east coast, the Florida panther became one of the first species added to the US Endangered Species List in 1973. Back then the problem was hunting, these days the problem is habitat destruction. Today there are less than a hundred Florida panthers in the wild. In the nineties that number was as low as thirty, close to extinction, but in 1995, eight female pumas were brought in from Texas to strengthen the population numbers and gene pool. It worked. Sort of. Sustainable recovery is proving extraordinarily difficult. The Californian mountain lion population (roughly five thousand) is healthy by comparison, but inbreeding is beginning to take its toll. While the numbers suggest a healthy population the truth is much more fraught.

So. P-22. He is now a bona fide Hollywood celebrity (he's hung out underneath the house of Brad Pitt's neighbour, and acquired both a Twitter handle and a Facebook page; he's a soft toy). What he doesn't have, of course (to quote various articles), is a 'girlfriend'. He has expanded his territory but there are no females nearby. At twenty square kilometres Griffith Park is about a twentieth the size of a male mountain lion's desired territory, and he shares this territory with five million human visitors a year. And so he roams, late at night, alone. He's seven now, and given that his life expectancy is ten, the odds that he'll mate and procreate are lengthening.

Some mammals, however, are adapting and evolving to be suited to urban environments, and it's possible they are even developing into new species. The Eurasian blackbird (*Turdus merula*) differentiated sufficiently—in certain urban environments where it enjoys warmer temperatures, abundant food scraps and freedom from predators—to constitute a new species, which Menno Schilthuizen, the author of *Darwin Comes to Town: How the Urban Jungle Drives Evolution*, calls *Turdus urbanicus*. 'The constellation of European cities has become urban evolution's Galápagos, and *Turdus merula* its Darwin's finch.'[1] Schilthuizen also quotes research on the London Underground mosquito, which has not just evolved into a new form, but is also genetically distinct depending on which tube line you're on: the Central, the Bakerloo or the Victoria.

But new species are not evolving at anywhere near the same rate as we're losing them. And, more tragically for P-22, because he has not been able to mate, any genetic advantage that enabled him to negotiate the freeways won't be passed on. 'Pumas in areas like the Santa Monicas, the Santa Anas

---

1 'The Concrete Jungle', David Quammen, *New York Review of Books*, November 8, 2018.

and especially the postage stamp of Griffith Park, are betting against the house. In the long run, the house always wins.'[2]

P-22's aloneness strikes me (though probably not him) as more existential because he's been wearing a GPS collar since 2012. According to the *LA Times*,[3] this beams his location eight times a day via satellite to one of twenty-four ground stations around the world, and then on to a computer in Berlin that researchers access from an office in Thousand Oaks.

He tends to move around the park in a seven-day cycle, often coming very close to roads and houses and the humans who inhabit them. That is why, I assume, he ended up in a crawl space in a house next to a property once owned by Brad Pitt. A friend and I decided to visit the house. We parked down the hill, then wound our way up a canyon rim, lined by houses that overlook the park. I was struck by how steep the slope into (or out of) the park was; I tried to imagine what it would have been like for P-22 to stalk up this hill and curl up under a house, only to wake up to being pelted with tennis balls and photographed by paparazzi. Less glamorously, he's also survived a serious bout of illness after eating rat poison. (Eighty-five per cent of mountain lions and seventy per cent of wildlife tested in California in recent years have been exposed to dangerous rodenticides. In 2016 alone, more than 4,400 small human children became ill after eating poison intended for rodents.)

---

2   UC Davis biologist Walter Boyce, quoted in 'A week in the life of P-22, the big cat who shares Griffith Park with millions of people', Thomas Curwen, *Los Angeles Times*, February 8, 2017.

3   Curwen.

P-22 has always known that being seen is a bad thing: is evasive for that very reason. But on this trip I found I was thinking more seriously about that experience: being looked at. Some women talk about how painful they find the invisibility that descends once you're a certain age, but I began to enjoy mine. At fifty-two, in a country where no one knew me, I could pull on my invisibility like Harry Potter's cloak. Eyes down, exaggerate the middle-aged stoop and—*Shazam!*— you're safe. Relatively. Kim Novak, who played Madeline in *Vertigo*, has talked about identifying with her role in that film. The way Hollywood tried to make her over for the audience's gaze. You would think, at age eighty-three, the work of being looked at was over, but the President of the United States recently suggested that Novak should sue her plastic surgeon, so apparently not. Novak enjoyed working with Hitchcock though, famously, Tippi Hedren—who, coincidentally, owned several lions—did not.

Anyway. There is a wonderful photo of a mountain lion taken in Ronald W. Caspers Wilderness Park in 1986. Doug Schulthess took a photo of his wife Loye and her small daughter Natalie while they were hiking. Loye stands with her toddler, beaming, the barren hills jutting up behind her. If you look closely, behind a couple of thorny shrubs and some tufts of grass you see a mountain lion's face, the eyes glinting ever so slightly.

This is what P-22 knew: it is predators who do the looking, prey who are looked at.

Cameras still seek out P-22 and indeed I first learned

about him after surveillance cameras captured a picture of him prowling around the Los Angeles Zoo the night a koala was taken. 'While zoo cameras did not capture P-22 in the act, officials said there was ample evidence to support their belief that the big cat found his way into the marsupial enclosure before making off with the koala.' Parts of Killarney's mangled body were found a short distance away.

The zoo itself did not make a fuss about the killing. It acknowledged the dangers of sitting snug against a relative wilderness, and after I visited the koala exhibit at the zoo I understood how easy the strike would have been. The fencing between the park and the zoo is patchy: some sections are failing or have collapsed altogether. Killarney lived in a sunken pit with a low fence—easy for P-22 to get into, although getting out of the pit with a koala in his mouth would have been a challenge. 'Australia' House at the LA Zoo was not, as described on the website, a series of enclosures, 'brimming with change as kangaroo and koala joeys' emerged 'from their mothers' pouches' and explored 'their new habitat'. The Nocturnal House, which featured a 'rare' southern hairy-nosed wombat, had an atmosphere that brought Bardo to mind, lacking even the stylish panache of the deserted shopping malls that litter the US. The website mentioned something about the shade of *Eucalyptus* trees but what I saw was that, despite the eucalypts that abound in Griffith Park, Killarney was kept in a concrete enclosure with a dead trunk in the middle to which (I assume) leafy branches were tied at mealtimes. Koalas at the Healesville Sanctuary are also fed by tying leaves to fake trees but they are, at the same time, surrounded by living ones.

I don't dismiss the notion that zoos have a role in a world that is both expanding and shrinking. But the use of animals in what appear to be marketing campaigns for zoos with inadequate facilities is distressing. Back in Australia, of course, koalas are struggling in the wild and their population sits at a single per cent of what it was before white settlement. They are the butt of jokes about chlamydia, which is killing them in large numbers. They are starving to death as deforestation lays waste to much of the east coast of Australia. The koala's current classification is 'threatened' but, as Lyndon Schneiders, director of the Wilderness Society pointed out recently, there are five hundred Australian animals on that list and most of them will find themselves on another list in the not-at-all-distant future: 'extinct'.[4] If Australia's Endangered Species Act doesn't become more substantive, it's estimated that koalas will be gone from the wild by 2050. Which leaves koalas like Killarney at the mercy of zoos.

In the early morning after that visit to Los Angeles Zoo I walked through Griffith Park. When I'm in LA I try to stay close enough to it that I can visit most mornings. On a clear day—and this was such a day—you look down across the city. To my left was the empty Silver Lake Reservoir, drained in 2015 as part of a project to build a bypass pipeline. The Los Angeles River sparkled as it flowed, more strongly than it had for some years, through its concrete canyon. The drought that

---

4   'Fears for the future of Australia's koalas', *RN Breakfast*, ABC, December 14, 2018.

struck the state in 2010 was over, but California was trying to prepare for the possibility of permanent drought, for it has become the state bearing the brunt of climate change, both literal (a boom and bust cycle of floods, drought, bushfire) and in terms of policy development. As President Trump isolates the US from any global policy initiatives and downgrades organisations such as the EPA, California's Governor Jerry Brown is meeting with China's chief climate negotiator, and has announced plans for California and China to work together on zero-emissions vehicles and fuel-cell research.

As I meandered my way up a path that took me to the park's northern section I smelled the lemon-scented gums before I saw them. Glorious. Afficionados will know that #treeoftheday April 7, 2016 was a lemon-scented gum. Two, in fact. They were planted ninety years ago by either Walter Burley or Marion Griffin—no one seems to know who—after the completion of Newman College at Melbourne University. The trees' skin glows as if lit from within. Their boughs swing low, heavy with long, narrow leaves, with gumnuts and blossom. Woody patches of bark nestle in their elbows and knees. Their fragrance drifts through peak-hour traffic.

The latin name of the lemon-scented gum is now *Corymbia citriodora*, though until the early 1990s it was *Eucalyptus citriodora*. Some naturalists and scientists still insist that is the correct nomenclature.

One of the main difficulties facing plant classifiers is deciding upon acceptable criteria and ranges of variation in characteristics. Of course, this problem stems from the fact that any biological classification is a man-made scheme into which we try to fit a whole range of living things, primarily for our own convenience of organisation—which is not to say there is no rigour to the process.[5]

All up, 113 trees were moved out of the genus *Eucalyptus* into the genus *Corymbia*, including the bloodwoods and ghost gums. Once you know what to look for, you see they look more like an *Angophora* (also a genus) than a *Eucalyptus*. Both genera have smooth skin in a variety of fleshy tones, and their beautiful limbs are as reminiscent of tendrils as of branches.

It was Rebecca Giggs who pointed out to me that Australian newspapers use 'that' for animals. The Associated Press style manual stipulates: '"who" is only appropriate when an animal has been given a personal name.' If the tree I'm writing about has an individual name—some do—I use it. I assign pronouns like he and she, when that seems right. Time and time again, when trying to identify my #treeoftheday I've started out asking myself, 'What is this tree called?' and ended up wondering what's in a name. From there it is a slippery slope down into the mire of language and meaning. I become philosophical, read my Dao: 'Naming is the origin of all particular things.'

All this leads me to wonder: is a Florida puma still

---

5 *Native Trees and Shrubs of South-eastern Australia*, Leon Costermans, Reed New Holland, 2009, p. 2.

a Florida puma if Texan pumas have been bred into the population? Is P-22 an appropriate name for a heroic mountain lion? What does Killarney mean? Does it matter that I think of lemon-scented gums as *Eucalyptus* when they are *Corymbia*?

It was on this day, a day of thinking about the wild animals that are being forced into the cities and the ways in which they survive, a day of wondering how to write about P-22 and Killarney, a day when I saw my favourite gums bending in a gentle breeze above Los Angeles, that my brother called.

We drove back to San Francisco. I stayed one night, then got on a plane. Fourteen hours later, after a combination of sleeping pill, vodka and bad movies, I stood in a series of lines at Sydney airport trying to make my flight to Melbourne. The lines were long. I was going to miss my connection. I finally blurted out something about Dad's imminent death, a card I had not wanted to play; but I did play it, and it worked, and they moved me to the front of the line. My brother picked me up from the airport and we drove to the home Dad had been living in for two years. My uncle sat by his dying brother. When I arrived he said, 'I've been keeping him alive for you,' then stepped outside for a break. A few hours later Dad died. There were four of us there. I'd been told many stories about people needing to be alone to die but I knew that was not what Dad would have wanted. He liked his people around him. If he'd been a tree he'd have needed a forest.

His decline was unspeakably grim. I can find no silver lining in it. (Will you write about your dad's dementia? people ask me. What would I say? I reply.) But here is the thing. Being with him when he died, that was the silver lining. It was an honour. A privilege. My brother, Dad's brother, Dad's wife, me—we had loved him, he had loved us. We forgot, for a while at least, all the rest.

YELLOWWOOD

YELLOWWOOD

(*Cladrastis kentukea*)

When the frost comes out in the spring, and even in a
thawing day in the winter, the sand begins to flow down the
slopes like lava, sometimes bursting out through the snow and
overflowing it where no sand was to be seen before.

HENRY DAVID THOREAU

FROM where I was sitting in Bloomington, Indiana, the
northern hemisphere's spring looked like it would
never come. The trees were skeletal, and my attempts
at identification usually failed. I gave up and called
everything an oak or occasionally a chestnut. The sleet
and snow continued into late April. I found it hard to

believe that it was a warmer winter than usual but people kept insisting it was so, and the stories weren't just anecdotal. Other countries in the north were reporting similar warming. The frozen soils Nordic foresters rely on were thawing, turning forest floors into mud and swallowing the massive equipment used to harvest timber. When I first heard that, I fist-pumped the air—*Go Trees!*—before I thought through the disturbing implications of melting permafrost. More stored carbon being released into the air; 'zombie microbes' such as anthrax, the collapse of permafrost ecosystems.

Spring's arrival was less predictable and its duration shorter than it once had been, but arrive it did, and suddenly I could tell a birch from a beech from an oak from a maple. I came to understand that sycamores and planes are basically the same tree.

People had gone out of their way to detail the bleakness of America's Midwest. This had the happy effect of making me very grateful for the beauty around me in southern Indiana. There are lots of stories I could tell about Indiana and trees, the most famous being the one about Johnny Appleseed, who sailed along the Ohio River, moving through the Midwest planting apples, but it's a story Michael Pollan tells so well I'll leave it to him.[1] As often as I could, which was not often enough, I drove to Brown County State Park. Shafts of sunlight cut between stands of trees, their fallen leaves forming a crunchy brown carpet underfoot. Golden creek beds ran through clefts in the undulating valleys. The soundtrack to this dramatic landscape

---

1 *The Botany of Desire*, Michael Pollan, Random House, 2001.

was the constant whisper of the beech leaves, which dry but don't drop, and rustle whenever the breeze picks up.

These modest gorges and escarpments were carved by glacier melt. Sixteen thousand years ago fast-moving glaciers reached down from Alaska as far as central Indiana, the weight of the ice planing the grand prairies to the north and the tumultuous runoff carving the hills and valleys to the south. That is where some of America's great forests formed. Some millennia later the ecosystem is described in the literature as oak-hickory mix.

As early as 1915 the area's potential as a park had been noted.

The state of Indiana should buy as much of Brown County as possible. It should acquire at least 1,000 acres in the wildest part of the county. The heart of Brown County is purely wild...From the scenic standpoint, Brown County is one of the best spots that ever existed in the great stretch between the Appalachians and the Rocky Mountains.[2]

After several generations of farming, the fragile earth had degraded and eroded to the point it was unusable for agriculture, and so a bill was passed by the state legislature that allowed counties to give tracts of land to the state for state parks. Brown County State Park opened in 1929 in the southern area of Indiana that is home to one of the rarest

---

2   ourbrowncounty.com

and most spectacular trees in the eastern United States: the yellowwood.

One afternoon I walked with friends through one of the remaining stands of yellowwood in the park. As we negotiated the steep steps into the ravine we passed hickory shag bark, American beech, sassafras, dogwood. Tiny orchards. We saw two different types of snake; many squirrels. The stand of young, whip-thin yellowwood were not clearly distinguishable from the beech, to my untrained eye, though the difference would have been obvious if they were in bloom. If you're there at the right time of year (we were not) the trees fold over with the weight of fronds that look like giant pea flowers, which is what they are: the tree is, in fact, a legume. Without the flowers, I had to rely on the cheerful wave of the pink researcher's flags to identify it. The yellowwood is erratically distributed due to the to-ing and fro-ing of glaciers over several ice ages. This stand and the population at nearby Yellowwood State Forest are the northernmost stands left, isolated from friends in Kentucky, 160 kilometres away. The tree is increasingly endangered (though not listed as such in Kentucky). In 2018 the Yellowwood State Forest was opened to logging, which explained why most gardens in the town of Bloomington had weathered-looking signs jammed into the soil: *Save Yellowwood*.

One day when I was in the park I talked at length to a local naturalist named David. He was a kind, knowledgeable man who tolerated an endless torrent of questions from me about local trees. He was, I realised, doing his best to be as optimistic as a man can be when he cares about the environment under late-stage capitalism in a state that has thrown in its lot with Mike Pence. An hour of conversation ranged across the overuse of pesticides, chestnut blight (the tree species is not yet extinct, but several invertebrate species closely associated with the American chestnut now are), dieback in American ash and the now-endangered Indiana brown bat (its caves are being disturbed by humans; a fungus known as white-nose syndrome is killing the remnant populations). At this time of year the sunset stretched out to 9 p.m., long after the chill of evening had descended. As I became colder, I caught David's eye and it seemed to me we were both trying not to give in to the tears threatening to spill. Research supports much of what he was telling me, and what I could see with my own eyes every time I walked through a forest. Milder winters have allowed many species of bark beetles to proliferate, forestry practices favour particular beetle-susceptible tree species. Deadly fungus and disease evolve at a far greater rate than a tree can manage. The trees aren't living long enough to fight back.[3]

I farewelled David—I stay in touch with him on Facebook—and walked to my car. As I was about to get in, I saw a massive turkey vulture spilling out of a garbage bag a metre or so away: dumped after being (illegally) shot. I got down on my haunches and sat for a while in the dying light, admiring the strangeness of the red folds of skin on its head;

---

3 'The ecology, distribution, conservation and management of large old trees', David B. Lindenmayer and William F. Laurance, *Biol. Rev.* (2017), 92, pp. 1434–58.

deeply impressed by the heft of its enormous shoulders and wings. These birds are so much larger and grander than they seem when you're a mere mortal standing on the earth, neck craned back, watching vultures cruise the thermals above you, rulers of the sky.

FORT. DA!

FORT. DA!

WHEN I was researching my book on Cyclone Tracy back in 2012, I visited Kakadu National Park in the Northern Territory during the build-up, that time when humidity hovers around ninety per cent and clouds hang so low and heavy in the sky you feel you could reach into them. It's a cheaper time to travel, but you have to be keen. One morning I got up at dawn and walked the half-hour to Nourlangie Rock. It wasn't far but by the time I got there I was a veritable thunderstorm myself, sweat sheeting off me. I waded, rather than walked, through space. When I got to the caves I saw the painting of one of the first sailing ships to reach this area about two hundred years ago. The white sails billowed. It's the kind of art that collapses time, that makes you see the world differently. There are more first-contact paintings at Ubirr gallery, which was (for me) a drive away. White men in their outlandish trousers with their pipes and hats. Most of the art in this area is older. It dates from around fifteen hundred years ago and is painted in a traditional Arnhem Land style known as X-ray art because of the cross-hatching that depicts the bones of the barramundi, wallabies, goanna. But the painting that really stopped me in my tracks was fainter, more a blur of iron red bleeding into the rock. A thylacine.

It's been three thousand years since thylacine have lived on mainland Australia. Dingoes are name-checked in their extinction here because the thylacine died out soon after the dingo arrived in the later part of the Holocene. This was a time of decreasing summer rain and temperatures, alongside increasing winter rain. Sea levels were rising. This changing climate, drier but with more floods, was a challenge for the strange and beautiful creatures, and must share some of the blame for the thylacine's demise. I say strange because thylacine didn't look anything like *Canis*, *Vulpes*, *Panthera* or any other big cats and dogs. They looked like marsupials. They had stiff sticky-outy tails, tiger-like stripes, broad foreheads and long pointy noses. They sometimes hopped. Their powerful jaws could hinge 120 degrees, and they made a yipping sound rather than barking or howling.

I know what a thylacine looks like because of the devastating footage I saw of the last one in captivity, a thylacine called Benjamin, running back and forth in his enclosure in 1933. Bounty had been paid on more than two thousand of his kin—seven shillings for females, five shillings for males. On July 10, 1936 Tasmania listed the thylacine as a protected species, but the political intervention came far too late. That pattern—too little and too late—continues to this day.

Back. Forth.

When I think of that footage, I find myself thinking of Sigmund Freud's description of repetitive games played by children to help them overcome fear and establish the illusion of mastery. He described his grandson Ernst's 'occasional disturbing habit of taking any small objects he could get hold of and throwing them away from him into a corner, under the bed', and saying *Fort* (gone) with some satisfaction. Other games involved tying a reel to a piece of string, throwing it— *Fort*—and then pulling it back into view. *Da* (there).

On September 7, 1936, some 30 million years after the fossil record suggests thylacine first walked the earth, Benjamin was left out of his enclosure one cold night and died of exposure. At the board meeting following Benjamin's death the Hobart Zoo set aside thirty pounds to replace him.

Da!

Only to discover that no more thylacine were to be found. *Fort.*

There continue to be reported sightings and rewards offered for evidence that thylacine still exist. This strikes me as an extraordinary act of denial. I don't mean to suggest it's impossible they might, but I wonder, what is the point of proving some remnant populations have survived if it's only to bring them back to our dangerous attention? Might their paws not be hacked off, their carcasses hung off fences? Will they be stuck in zoos and left, once more, to die of cold? Will tourists swarm through their territory in the hope of seeing them?

The biggest killer on the planet of animals, of any species, is humans. We view other predators as competition—and I suppose, if you're a farmer looking after stock, they are. But we're terrified of them. Beyond reason. The Tasmanian Government recently spent 50 million dollars to eradicate foxes, even though it's unclear whether there *is* a fox population on the island.[1] There's a certain amount of concern for marsupials, but it's the rights of stock and those who own them that have driven much of our political agenda.

One attempt at such protections is the longest fence in the world, Australia's dingo fence. It runs for 5614 kilometres, meandering, much as a waterway might, from the Great Australian Bight to the Darling Downs north of Brisbane. The point of the dingo fence is to keep the dingo out of southeastern Australia and protect the sheep therein. James Woodford is a journalist who has travelled the entire fence, and his book

---

1 'Paper Tiger', Brooke Jarvis, *New Yorker*, July 2, 2018.

The Dog Fence describes graphically the corpses of hundreds of camels and entire mobs of emus that have died searching for water during drought.[2] Collateral damage. The fence is draped with the carcasses of dead dingoes, minus the bits of them removed to claim bounty.

The pastoralists along some areas of the fence have tolerated being used as missile and nuclear testing sites and mined for uranium. They have suffered through endless drought and struggled to manage soil erosion due to over-grazing. Dingoes are not the big problem here. And while it is true that dingoes kill sheep, research suggests that in areas where dingoes are shot and poisoned, livestock predation goes up, not down. This is in part because dingoes keep feral cat, fox and pig numbers down. But it's also because dingoes that grow up with their family structures intact hunt more strategically. Adults train the juveniles to hunt more skilfully and to understand their territory, which means their behaviour is less erratic and destructive. Some cattle pastoralists want dingoes to be able to roam freely, believing they lose more of their stock to starvation when the animals are competing with kangaroos for pasture. Dingoes that have grown up with their families know how to form a mob and bring a kangaroo down. Introduced deer, too, are becoming a problem in southeastern Australia (just as they are in areas where wolves have disappeared). If dingoes were allowed through these lands they would help sort that out. The loss of predators is creating problems in ecosystems around the word.

2   *The Dog Fence*, James Woodford, Text Publishing, 2003.

The Australian dingo has lived on the Australian continent for four thousand years or more, and is believed to have crossed the land bridges that existed between Indonesia and Australia. Academic and author Deborah Bird Rose observes:

> Dingoes provided a companionship that had never before existed in Australia. These creatures were the first non-humans who answered back, came when called, helped in the hunt, slept with people and learned to understand some of the vocabulary of human languages…People gave them names, fitted them into the wider kinship structure and took care of dead dingoes in the same way they took care of dead people. Dingoes have been fitted into the sacred geography as extremely powerful Dreamings, and they now figure prominently in ritual, songlines and stories.[3]

Settler Australians sometimes refer to the dingo as introduced, which is a bit rich. It's also self-serving. A native dingo might be worth saving; an introduced wild dog, not so much. But for any variety of reasons the dingo is now classified as vulnerable in the wild and is, according to some, close to extinction, in part because of interbreeding with domestic dogs to which they are related, but not, genetically speaking,

---

3   *Wild Dog Dreaming: Love and Extinction*, Deborah Bird Rose, University of Virginia Press, 2011.

identical. It is difficult to distinguish hybrids from pure dingoes and the actual population numbers are not known, but it's believed that more than a third of southeastern Australia's dingoes are hybrids. Hybrids have, historically, made humans uncomfortable and are often 'eradicated'.

In the northern hemisphere coyotes have been interbreeding with domestic dogs, and with red wolves. Such was the concern that the red wolf would become impure that hybrids began to be slaughtered. This hasn't saved them from their inevitable extinction—at the time of writing there were fifty red wolves left.

Hybrids present a particular problem when it comes to legal policy, particularly in the USA where the Endangered Species Act has been described as 'almost eugenic'[4] because it excludes hybrids from protection. Sometimes it's not even clear if the interbreeding is between two different species at all. It's a long story and Dan Flores, the author of *Coyote America*, tells it well. But, long story short, coyotes are red wolves, give or take geography and a few thousand years of separate breeding, virtually indistinguishable genetically speaking. Between a wolf and a dog. The animals mate because they recognise each other. They mate because humans have disturbed the environment in such a profound way that coyotes have migrated east, desperate to get away from the legislated slaughter of their kind. Riding the boundary line of genetic purity is an ongoing issue in times like these, when we fear losing species, but to insist on it is the same as insisting that

---

4   *Europe: A Natural History*, Tim Flannery, Text Publishing, 2018, p. 158.

human beings of different species didn't mate when there is an increasing body of evidence that they did, and that the result was European humans.[5] Other mammals, such as the golden jackal and the wisent (or European bison) are, basically, hybrids.

Hybridisation can be a form of evolution, and there is no doubt that the urbanisation of the planet (alongside climate change) is creating a series of pressures on fauna to adapt and evolve very quickly. Some hybrids struggle to reproduce, but others display traits popularly known as hybrid vigour, which, if they *can* reproduce, is useful in an adaptive sense.

The grey wolf was one of the most widely distributed wild mammals in the northern hemisphere, in part because it can tolerate a wide range of climates. They now occupy about two-thirds of their former range worldwide, and about ten per cent of their historic range in the USA, where there are estimated to be six thousand left (sixteen thousand if you include Alaska). The release of fourteen grey wolves into Yellowstone National Park in 1995 is a much touted good news story that certainly illustrates the positive effects of allowing predators back into the system. Elk numbers are down, which means that a greater diversity of plants can thrive. This, in turn, benefits the grizzly bears. Hare and beaver numbers are up and, as a consequence, bald eagle numbers. On it goes, the trophic cascade, rippling, powerful, driving down through the ecosystem like a waterfall.

As well as its numbers improving in the US, the grey wolf is returning to parts of Europe after a period of extinction. In

---

5   Flannery, 2018, pp. 178 ff.

general, when I'm looking for good news stories, it's in Europe that I find them. Bison returning to Romania, wolves thriving in France, bears in Scandinavia. I asked a Finnish friend of mine if she'd ever seen a wolf and she said yes, she had, far off in the distance. She elaborated: the Finns also love wolverines, lynxes and bears unless they live close to them. People from the city love the idea of them, she said (and George Monbiot argues), but those who have to live with them are more fearful. This, despite the fact that a wolf hasn't killed a person in Finland in more than a hundred years. Wild boar were hunted to extinction in Britain some three hundred years ago and they, too, are making a comeback, having staged their own prison breaks (they are farmed as heritage livestock). Fabulously, they pose quite a legal problem as they are designated as variously 'dangerous', 'non-native' and 'wild', each designation providing different protections to the boar. To kill a dangerous and non-native animal is allowed. Killing a wild animal is not. Best of all, boars don't just tear up legislation, they tear up the soil as they root around for food. This is great for plant diversity, but not so great for church lawns.

Coyote have proved more resilient than wolves when it comes to surviving the relentless slaughter of the last hundred years. They have extended their range out of the western deserts where they once thrived as far north as Alaska and across to cities on the eastern seaboard. Only human beings have managed to extend their range as quickly and widely. 'Southwestern Hispanos have a rich folk tradition about coyotes and have long said the only thing smarter than a coyote is God.'[6] I've seen them myself in Joshua Tree National Park. Trotting along. Flopping down into the cooling sand of an evening and gnawing on jack rabbits while throwing you the occasional glance, insolent as teenagers. Virginia saw one that was somewhat shyer early one morning on Bernal Heights. Seventy breeding pairs live in San Francisco. It's not known how many live in Los Angeles, though is undoubtedly a larger number than that, and some 145 are currently being tracked there by the National Park Service, who are trying to understand how they can live in such a fragmented environment.

The Animal Damage Control Act was passed in 1931 with the stated aim of total eradication of coyote. The poisonous baits that were left out to kill them in numbers approaching the millions took other animals as well. Eagles, bears, domestic pets. You name it, the poison kills it. Richard Nixon banned the use of strychnine, thallium sulphate and cyanide for the poisoning of coyotes, declaring, 'The old notion that "the only good predator is a dead one" is no longer acceptable.'

Pesticides don't just poison the trees but also the soil and the plants that spring up once the trees are gone. They poison the animals that eat those plants. They're an environmental disaster, a disaster that was first recognised when Rachel Carson's *Silent Spring* was published back in 1962.[7]

---

6   *Coyote America*, Dan Flores, Basic Books, 2016, p. 23.

7   First published in the *New Yorker*, and then as a book. The book is out of print, but the *New Yorker* articles can still be read online: www.newyorker.com/magazine/1962/06/16/silent-spring-part-1

There had been several sudden and unexplained deaths, not only among the adults but also among the children, who would be stricken while they were at play, and would die within a few hours. And there was a strange stillness. The birds, for example—where had they gone? Many people, baffled and disturbed, spoke of them. The feeding stations in the back yards were deserted. The few birds to be seen anywhere were moribund; they trembled violently and could not fly. It was a spring without voices.

The use of pesticides has become more widespread since Carson wrote those words, and the spring steadily more silent. 'It's estimated that there are 421 million fewer birds in Europe in 2009 than there had been in 1980…very large declines in the volume of insects have been recorded.'[8] Half of the species of bees in Germany are close to extinction, a country in which eighty per cent of its plants (which includes food) rely on bees as pollinators. All the Midwesterners I spoke to on my most recent trip to the US—a cohort often described as conservative on these matters—were extremely concerned about pesticide use.

In her *Quarterly Essay* 'Us and Them', Anna Krien refers to the biologist Edward O. Wilson's description of the period that will follow the mass extinction of species that is currently taking place as 'The Age of Loneliness'. It's the kind of phrase

---

8   Flannery, 2018, pp. 294–5.

that chimes out, and leaves a deep silence in its place. What does extinction sound like? Wind sweeping across land denuded of trees? I suspect that it sounds like the world did after Cyclone Tracy wiped out much of Darwin:

> No sounds at all—no birds, no frogs, nothing, I think that was one of the things that hit us more than anything else, was that there was not a sound of anything which you would normally associate with the wet season, like cicadas or birds or frogs— nothing, absolutely nothing.[9]

Bernie Krause, once a composer of film scores, including *Apocalypse Now*, has been recording the sounds of nature for fifty years. He is described as a soundscape ecologist. That project has evolved/devolved into one in which he has recorded the sounds of extinction through America.

> When I began recording over four decades ago, I could record for ten hours and capture one hour of usable material, good enough for an album or a film soundtrack or a museum installation. Now, because of global warming, resource extraction and human noise, among many other factors, it can take up to 1,000 hours or more to capture the same thing. Fully fifty per cent of my archive comes from habitats so radically altered that they're either altogether silent or

---

9 *Warning: The Story of Cyclone Tracy*, Sophie Cunningham, Text Publishing, 2014.

can no longer be heard in any of their original form.[10]

There is, of course, a lot of human noise to fill in the silence, and yet another issue is that bats, birds and other creatures struggle to be heard over the din. Air conditioners, industrial machines, planes, helicopters, cars. The list is long. This human noise is known as anthrophony and it competes with natural sounds, known as biophony.

Krause has given examples of the ways in which human sound drowns out nature's sounds, and how this can lead, in turn, to more sounds of silence. The Great Basin spadefoot toad digs itself down each winter, about a metre under the hard-packed desert soil of the American West. In the spring, when there's enough moisture both in the soil and pooling into puddles on top of it, the toads will dig themselves to the surface and gather around the temporary water sources. They then launch into a harmonious chorus: both because they're looking for mates, and because if they vocalise in sync it makes it difficult for predators like coyotes to single out any individual for a meal. Recently, however, one of their habitats has been favoured by US Navy jet pilots flying over at speeds greater than 1100 kilometres an hour only a couple of hundred metres above ground level. Krause found that the noise masked the sound of the chorusing toads so they couldn't harmonise. After each fly-by, it took the toads forty-five minutes to resume their chorusing—during which time, under a full moon, Krause watched as two coyotes came in to pick them off.

---

10 'The Voice of the Natural World', Bernie Krause, TED Talk, August 27, 2014.

You can listen, if you are brave enough, to the final chittering of the last Christmas Island pipistrelle bat as it calls, searching for others of its kind. It received no reciprocal call and was never heard from again. Scientists warned the federal government about the 'looming catastrophe',[11] but the government prevaricated—back and forth, back and forth—for three years, by which time it was too late.

Da!

Fort!

Thirty-five per cent of all global mammal extinctions since 1500 have been Australian, and ten per cent of all reptile extinctions. That is thirty out of eighty-four worldwide. We have the worst mammal extinction rate in the world and a massive 1700 species of our animals and plants are listed by the Australian Government as being at risk of extinction.[12] Federal laws have been put in place to protect the ecosystems of a host of rare species, but scientists recently took satellite data of forest and bushland that had been logged or bulldozed, and overlaid it with maps of threatened-species habitat. They found 7.6 million hectares of that habitat had been destroyed between 2000 and 2017. Animals particularly affected include the koala, cassowary, greater glider and several bird species. In the middle of 2018 the Senate opened an inquiry into the extinction crisis. Issues raised included poor monitoring of extant laws, cuts to environment department budgets, poor coordination between state and federal departments, failure

---

11   'Unmourned death of a sole survivor', Tim Flannery, *Sydney Morning Herald*,
November 17, 2012.

12   australianwildlife.org

to implement management plans—though less than forty per cent of our threatened species even *have* management plans—and a lack of accountability. Australia has not listed a critical habitat for protection on the federal register for more than a decade.[13] Whether this inquiry will lead to effective changes in a timely manner it's hard to tell. History suggests not.

Dan Flores writes that the yodel of the coyote is 'inseparable from the silvery wash of the planets and the high moons of winter night skies'.[14] James Woodford describes the dingo's yowl as 'haunting and beautiful'. Deborah Rose has

> heard the dingoes singing across the cliffs and gorges, across plains and deserts, and I cannot really comprehend that no matter how bright the night, or how sweet the air, there may come a day when we'll never hear them sing like that, ever. Not to their Sisters in the Sky country, or to the hunter in the Sky and on Earth, or for the love of their own kind, or in celebration of their own way of being in the world.[15]

The knowledge of our undoing flickers, as if in the periphery of my vision, and such a flicker comes to me unbidden. I am back—on another trip, in a drier season—in Kakadu National Park, driving back to the campsite at the

13 'Senate launches inquiry into threatened species "extinction crisis"', Lisa Cox, *Guardian*, June 27, 2018.

14 Flores, p. 137.

15 Rose, *Wild Dog Dreaming*.

misnamed South Alligator grounds. It's after dark. There is no moon. Dingoes race along the road's embankment and keep pace, momentarily, with the car. It's exhilarating. They are powerful and pale. Wild. Their paws move steadily over the red earth. Small fires lick all around us—it is burn-off time—and the flames light the dingoes' way through this darkest of nights.

OLIVE TREE

OLIVE TREE

(Olea europaea)

Of course, it helps to have a lot of money and clout. When I'm building and landscaping golf courses, I love to buy beautiful trees. Sometimes, though, those trees aren't in nurseries; sometimes they are in a person's backyard. I'll be driving down the highway, see a great tree, and ask my limo driver to pull over. I'll knock on the door. Usually, a woman will answer the door, and I'll say, 'Hi, lady. I'd love to buy your tree.' She'll say, 'Oh my god! It's Donald Trump! I can't believe this is happening!' And then I'll tell her that I'm building a golf course nearby…Usually, I'll get the tree. I've bought a lot of great trees that way…Money can't buy happiness, but it sure as hell can buy some great trees.

DONALD TRUMP, *Trump: Think Like a Billionaire*

A FRIEND recently confessed to me, quite seriously, that she had fallen in love with a tree and needed to spend some time with it every day, preferably lying under its full boughs. I did not find this strange, and the affair became all the more explicable when I learned the tree in question was an olive.

When I recently had the opportunity to stay in whitewashed Trulli, in an olive grove built on deep red soil, I was in tree heaven. The trees were heavily pruned to maximise productiveness. In Puglia olive crowns can be cropped *a cono*, *a cilindro*, *a vaso*, *a vaso polifinicos*, *a vaso cespugliato*. Farmers in northern Puglia prune trees so they resemble 'crooked old people, who have been frozen in a stop dance. Further south in Salento cropped olive crowns are formed like cups, letting plenty of light into the middle of the trees.'[1] That's what the trees were that surrounded us where we were staying in Ostuni: cups.

There are up to 60 million olive trees in Puglia, Italy, and they produce forty per cent of Italy's olive oil. About half a million of these trees are described as 'ancient', which means at least centuries old, and can mean millennia. These groves are the oldest and largest group of millenarian plants in the world. Gnarled, twisted, knotted, they are also well past their olive oil–producing prime. That is of no concern to tourists like me, but may explain why the trees are geotagged, a modern affectation made necessary by the trade in stolen ancient trees. These old unproductive trees not only take up space, they have to be pruned at regular intervals so it's possible that some farmers aren't totally aghast when they wake up one morning to find a huge hole where an ancient olive stood. The trees, which can fetch as much as twenty thousand Australian dollars on the black market, somehow find their way into the landscaped gardens of wealthy northern Italians. Similar thefts

---

1   italiannotes.com/pruning-olive-trees/

are occurring in Spain, Greece and Palestine. Puglia, though, is the first region to draft laws to protect the trees. There are steep fines for the removal of more than five trees per farm.

Olive trees are under attack on other fronts as well. A disease known as olive leaf scorch has affected thousands of hectares of olive plantations. Harvests in Italy are down by almost half. This is, of course, one of the major vulnerabilities of our oldest citizens. Old trees operate on a different time scale. They watch as entire human civilisations rise, then fall, as logging policies come and go, as species they once lived with are erased from the earth. And meanwhile fungi and pathogens come up with increasingly nimble ways to attack them. If humans could think in tree time they would not be stealing old olive trees, they would be planting new ones without concern for whether they would live to see them mature.

I saw the olives in the summer of 2018, at the beginning of a heatwave that went on to grip Europe for weeks. When in London I laughed along with other Australians about the notion that twenty-eight degrees could be considered dangerously hot, then descended to the Central line to catch the tube to Hampstead Heath. It was so hot in the train that I almost fainted. There's no air conditioning down there and by July the temperatures in some carriages were as high as forty degrees. Fires swept through Italy, Greece, Sweden and up into the Arctic Circle. Freshwater crays floated to the surface of the Finnish lakes, having suffocated because warmer water can't hold as much oxygen. In England long-hidden outlines known as crop marks revealed themselves as grass died and soil dried out: everything from Bronze Age fortifications to remnants of World War II infrastructure. These revelations are themselves a product of what has been described as our third world war, climate change. 'In the North this summer, a devastating offensive is underway. Enemy forces have seized huge swathes of territory; with each passing week, another 22,000 square miles [57,000 square kilometres] of Arctic ice disappears.'[2] Along the Elbe River in central Europe the water levels were so low that rocks known as Hunger Stones were rising to the surface. The oldest stone to emerge, carved in 1616, read, *When you see me, cry*.

2 'WW III is well underway, says environmentalist Bill McKibben', Arpan Bhattacharyya, *Big Think*, September 11, 2016.

BIYALA STORIES

BIYALA STORIES

A COUPLE of years ago I was standing on the banks of Moonee Ponds Creek, on Railway Canal in the gap between two overpasses, looking at several river red gums. The trees were still young, maybe twice my height; their pale green leaves a delicate spiderweb filtering the sky. They were at once scrappy and beautiful.

I was standing in this muddy place with a friend, a photographer, who told me they had germinated without human intervention from seeds washed down the creek; that, despite the fact the river red gum has the broadest natural distribution of any eucalypt, it was now rare for self-seeded trees to mature as these gums were doing.

Once common across the open woodlands of the land we call Melbourne, now they struggle for space in the urban environment. River red gums prefer creeks, wetlands and rivers—as do freeways, an engineering preference that has led to the concreting of waterways, the rerouting of rivers, and creeks being driven underground. The freeway runs overhead with Moonee Ponds Creek below. The creek used to be a chain of ponds—separate water bodies that linked up in times of heavy rain—and ran into the West Melbourne Swamp, once situated not far from where I was standing. After the draining of the swamp, the creek was rerouted via a series of drains to run some distance further, directly into the Yarra.

I saw these gums on a series of walks around Melbourne. It was over the months I did these walks that I came to realise that most of Melbourne's significant older trees, the ones that pre-dated white settlement, were river red gums or *Eucalyptus camaldulensis* (subspecies *camaldulensis*). The trees known as veterans were anything from four hundred to eight hundred years old. Some were dead but had been preserved and left standing as memorials: the Fairies Tree in Fitzroy Gardens, the Separation Tree in the Botanic Gardens, the Corroboree Tree at Burnley Oval.

Death is a mutable thing in trees. For a start, a tree's trunk, indeed all its wood, are dead cells. The life is in the thin sliver of living tissue on the outside of a tree. This is why ringbarking is so fatal. The final stage in a tree's life, the point when the rate of cell division lags behind the rate of cell death, is known as senescence. River red gums can remain in a state of senescence for more than a hundred years and what you might call a more active dying process can take about fifty years. Once dead, the skeletons of massive red gums continue to serve an ecological purpose. Many veteran gums are known as 'habitat' trees, because each tree, on average, supports an estimated sixteen mammals, forty-four birds and seven hundred insect species in the hollows created by fungus and fires, and by dropped limbs. That work continues long after the tree has 'died'.

In St Kilda Junction there is a living veteran, a twenty-metre-high river red gum known as the Ngargee Tree. When Queens Road was upgraded from a track to a road in 1875, it was diverted around the tree. The finest stand of river red gums I know of in Melbourne can be found on RMIT's Bundoora Campus. There is a ring, or fused tree, that lies on the ground now, but is still quite magnificent, a large weathered hoop where its limbs were tied together. That tree is just one of the more than a dozen veterans estimated to be eight hundred years old, including three canoe trees and the six Keelbundoora scarred trees. Scarred trees are trees that have had bark cut out of them to make anything from a coolamon to a large canoe or shelter. Keelbundoora was a Wurundjeri clan ancestor who was present at the signing of the Batman Treaty in 1835 (the treaty that purported to 'buy' Melbourne for some knives and shirts). Better known scarred trees exist in Treasury Gardens and Yarra Park. One of the two Yarra Park trees was recently presumed to be dead and was therefore cut back but, in a not-atypical red gum manoeuvre, it started to sprout from the base of its trunk and now has the growth patterns of a young tree, despite being several hundred years old. The second scarred tree has been standing there, exuding charisma, for anything up to eight hundred years and has been polished by the elements to a high silvery-grey sheen. Up close the bark is rough as an elephant's hide, and the line of the scar has curled to form a lip. The tree kept growing after the bark was removed, so the wood underneath is stretched taut and smooth. Archaeologist Gary Presland has argued that this particular scar is more likely to be the result of a fire crack than the excision of bark using stone axes.[1]

But whether scarred by fire or hatchet, a special connection exists between trees such as this and contemporary Wurundjeri people, a connection that 'underpins the high significance of these places. Once they are destroyed, the connection is largely destroyed.'[2] *Argus* journalist Howard Willoughby wrote as early as the 1880s that:

---

1   Presland, in conversation and in email exchange (January 24, 2017).

2   Wurundjeri Tribe Land and Compensation Council, quoted in 'Indigenous Cultural Heritage and History within the Metropolitan Melbourne Investigation Area', a report to the Victorian Environmental Assessment Council, Dr Shaun Canning and Dr Frances Thiele, February 2010, p. 23.

In the Yarra Park an inscription on a green tree calls attention to the fact that a bark canoe has been taken from the trunk. The canoe shape being evident in the stripped portion, and the marks of the stone hatchet being still visible on the stem. The blacks would find their way to the river impeded now by a treble-track railway that runs close to their old camp...[3]

Over in the Royal Botanic Gardens, there are two river red gums designated as significant by the National Trust. The more famous of them, the 400-year-old Separation Tree, stands on the site where citizens of Melbourne gathered on November 15, 1851 to celebrate the news that the colony of Victoria was to separate from New South Wales. The original Separation Tree was damaged in two separate ringbarking attacks in 2010 and 2013. After the first attack bridge grafting succeeded but the second attack undid that good work. By 2015 it was clear the tree was dying, so its canopy was slowly reduced. Vandals have attacked other veteran red gums as well. Development isolates these older trees, making them vulnerable: to diseases, to storms, to heat stress. The soil these lone trees grows in often becomes depleted. At the same time, the rarer the veterans become the more we value them.

We have left it too long to begin to replace our older trees. It can take hundreds of years for these trees to become old enough to support the insects, birds and mammals that rely

---

3 *Australian Pictures Drawn with Pen and Pencil*, Howard Willoughby, Religious Tract Society, London, 1886, p. 54.

on them. They have to be large enough, weathered enough, to have developed cavities.

> Individual large old trees and small stands of such trees can act as living 'micro-hotspots' with levels of species richness and individual species abundance substantially greater than the surrounding environment. Indeed, many species of animals occur in a given area only because of the presence of large old trees. Several studies have shown that patterns of nesting, denning and other social behaviour by cavity-dependent animals are dramatically altered when populations of large old trees are reduced.[4]

River red gums were felled in large numbers as Melbourne expanded—commercially harvested from around 1863—and it's hard to know how many were lost. Scientists have developed various estimates, all putting the numbers in the millions, but perhaps consider this. The wood of the river red gum is dense and is used for railway sleepers. About six hundred sleepers are used for a kilometre of track. Between 1864 and 1891, the railway networks of Victoria and New South Wales grew from 410 kilometres to 7650 kilometres.[5] That's just short of 4.5 million sleepers in twenty-seven years—and that is just one use the tree was put to.

---

4   'Conserving large old trees as small natural features', David B. Lindenmayer, *Biological Conservation*, 211 (2017), pp 51–9.

5   *Flooded Forest and Desert Creek: Ecology and History of the River Red Gum,* Matthew Colloff, CSIRO Publishing, 2014, p. 155.

These trees have not been replaced. Although there is now more consideration of these issues by councils and some policymakers, there will still be a gap of some two or three hundred years between the establishment of the new generation of trees into the old age in which they will contribute most to the ecosystem. It's in old age, too, that these trees hold the highest carbon load.

It was when I went to visit the Separation Tree that my relationship to the river red gum shifted from one of appreciation to a deeper curiosity. I noticed a second gum close by, one I hadn't read about. Like the Ngargee Tree, this second tree stood about twenty metres high, perhaps higher. I stopped in front of it and looked up into its thinning crown, its feathery pale green leaves sitting like lacework against a bright blue sky. Down lower it was lumpy and covered in burls. The river gum stood by the Ornamental Lake, once a swamp connected to the systems of wetlands around the Yarra River. When it germinated some centuries ago it would have been closer to the banks of the wandering river than it is today, and would have stood by while the Anderson Street (now Morell) Bridge was built—over dry land, before the Yarra River was rerouted beneath it. The tree would have felt, deep down in its roots, that the river was changing course, becoming shorter, straighter.

It is hard to convey the intensity this particular tree emanates as it stands, like a sentinel or an ancient god, looking across the land, without sounding slightly crazy. The publication of *The Secret Life of Plants* by Peter Tompkins back in 1973, which suggested that plants communicate with each other, was met with mockery. The author of the more recent *The Hidden Life of Trees*, Peter Wohlleben, argues something similar though he is more careful with his language. Of course there is an enormous leap between suggesting trees within a forest communicate with each other and that they communicate, like Tolkien's Ents, with other species. What I know is this. As I stood by the Ornamental Lake I found myself thinking: to understand Melbourne, its history, our environment, I need to know this tree.

Another way of putting this is that the tree came into focus. I saw something in it that was clear both to our first people and to some colonisers: these trees have practical uses at the same time as having a particular quality I'm going to describe, until a better, perhaps more accurate word, strikes me, as spiritual. Historian and author James Boyce saw this also.

> It is surely something of a miracle that such stupendous living connections with the Yarra world of 1835 have survived. There are two especially beautiful specimens in the Botanic Gardens around the lower lagoon, once part of the reserve in which the Kulin took early refuge before being expelled into less valuable swamps…I return to them often in my imagination because their roots, endurance, graceful hospitality, silent majesty and very survival seem to testify that…there is some force greater than us.[6]

---

6   James Boyce, *1835*, Black Inc., 2013.

That Baron Ferdinand von Mueller became such an eminent eucalyptus specialist leads me to believe that he too was struck by this tree and its kin. Certainly it's not just this particular eucalypt that projects this quality. Dr Matthew Colloff, author of a book on the history of the river red gum, spent ten years researching the ecology of the tree and its capacity to adapt to change. He writes, 'This tree connects time, place, people, land and water, desert and forest. The story is the history of our continent. The river red gum is central to that story.'[7]

River red gums are not just central to the story of this place, they inspire story. They have a powerful capacity for survival and you will find photos of river red gums flat out (like a lizard drinking), or fallen trees that have regenerated from a series of epicormic shoots reaching upwards from a horizontal trunk. When river red gum limbs drop or fire splits trunks and branches, sap heals the gash to protect the tree from fungus, and wound wood forms. When prolonged floodwaters threaten to drown them they can develop aerial roots. Their heartwood can burn or be eaten away, leaving their remnant lower trunks to form cathedral-like arches around a space that may be as large as a small room.

Questions are raised by most considerations of the river red gum, and those questions slip easily into narrative. During drought river red gums drop limbs suddenly, without warning; the occasional person has died as a result. Who was the person who died, what was their life like? How long has the drought

7   Colloff, p. 28.

been going that caused the tree to cast a limb? How much longer will that drought go on? Narrative formed when bark was cut to make a canoe for a river that ran a different course from the course it runs today. Or when the tree in the Royal Botanic Gardens provided temporary refuge for the Boon Wurrung and Wurundjeri who'd been driven out of central Melbourne. The narrative continues when that tree becomes the focus of political ceremony and is turned into a tourist attraction, and deepens, more tragically, when that tree is murdered. Ola Cohn's desire to carve the Fairies Tree in the early 1930s revealed a desire to turn the river red gum, quite literally, into a story, 'mostly for the fairies and those who believe in them, for they will understand how necessary it is to have a fairy sanctuary—a place that is sacred and safe as a home should be to all living creatures'. Personally, I'm struck by the moment in the 1840s when Melbourne's largest river gum—still standing—was used as a makeshift belfry for St Francis, Melbourne's oldest Catholic church, before being cut down in 1878 and carved into a throne for St Patrick's Cathedral. Prior to its execution, that tree was so big St Francis's planned expansions were impeded and the gum was described as 'terrorising' the church. After it became a throne it was sat on by Archbishop Mannix, a man who wielded significant political influence for forty-six years. More recently the controversial Cardinal Pell used it.[8] The author of *Tree Stories*, Peter Solness, became convinced the river gum 'was a

---

8   *Bearbrass*, Robyn Annear, Black Inc., 2005, p. 38.

genuine (if dormant) cultural icon, full of potential narrative'.[9] People would tell him stories about these trees, and about other trees, as he photographed them.

I've slipped here from the river red gum in particular to trees in general, but my point is that the river red gum provokes more stories than many beings do, sentient or otherwise. And we need its stories. 'Its innate toughness and capacity for survival inspire and motivate us. In the twenty-first century we need new narratives and new images of our connection with our land and waters, as well as respecting and celebrating those we already have.'[10]

I visited Barmah Lake, in the recently formed Barmah National Park on the border between Victoria and New South Wales, in early January. I wanted to see river red gums in a forest, not just as individual and ageing survivors. The Barmah-Millewa forest is a Ramsar site (a wetland of international importance), and at 71,575 hectares the largest river red gum forest still extant in the world. The reason the area has been saved from any development other than timber harvesting is that regular flooding makes the land unfit for pastoral use. That said, seasonal grazing has occurred over the last century, and wild horses run there still.

As I walk to Barmah Lake from the carpark, what first catches my eye is not the vertical lines of the thousands of young red gums reaching up to the light, but the horizontal ones:

9   Quoted by Colloff, p. 261.

10   Colloff, p. 261.

striations of greys, charcoal and ochre that delineate the levels of various inundations. Both the homogeneity of these trees' size, and their density, are the result of human intervention. They're resilient, but they can go for decades at a time without producing seedlings that mature. Both timber harvesting and grazing (with the consequent trampling of seedlings) have taken their toll on the tree's populations and, to quote Matt Colloff, 'Each phase of the forces of change has left its mark.'[11]

After extensive timber harvesting between the 1860s and the 1880s there was a massive regeneration event, one that produced an established stand of trees. Germination is always relatively straightforward but a seedling's journey to maturity is not. It requires a delicate balance of conditions, including a cycle of floods of the right depth and length of time, and more temperate conditions. Up to eighty per cent of the seedlings can survive but a two per cent survival rate is just as likely. By the 1960s full regeneration was occurring less and less frequently.

The stand that I was walking through now seemed to be an example of a successful, relatively recent regeneration event—quite possibly the one that occurred in 1974. I walked deeper into the forest to grassy woodland and there I began to see more of the increasingly rare veterans. I passed a river gum with looping fused branches, suggesting it had had its limbs tied together by the traditional owners of this land, the Yorta Yorta. There were various reasons this might be done, including marking tribal territory. I sat in the hollowed-out trunk of a habitat tree and admired the smooth charcoal of

---

11   Colloff, p. 254.

its walls, the light filtering in through the doorways. As I got closer to the lake the veterans began to cluster in larger numbers; presumably the variable water line had made them harder to get to. High roots fanned outwards in sturdy swirls that gave way to other root systems as they hit their neighbours' territory. The forces of (unnatural) selection meant many of these veterans were fabulously monstrous: thick, squat, misshapen, covered in burls. Loggers had preferred their straighter, neater siblings.

At the lake I stood near some large rushes (natives that are thriving in the changing conditions, pushing out the more fragile plants) and looked across the lake. My hiking boots sank slowly into the mud. Normally you'd expect it to be uncomfortably hot—it's often more than forty degrees here in summer—but it was a mild twenty-three and the rain was misting down upon me.

It wasn't only the river red gums that I noticed but the cracked mud of receding water, rotting gum leaves, greater eastern egrets, kingfisher, heron, ibis, ducks, emus, kangaroos, wild horses, wasps and flies. I even saw some Murray cod (critically endangered, because they've been overfished and the weirs don't suit them) foraging in the shallows near the bank, and learned to look for them at the centre of ripples of golden tannin. It was the first time I'd seen them surface in this amphibian-like manner. The effect was prehistoric. A single galah feather caught in a spiderweb stretched, strong as rope, between two river gums, waved gently in the corner of my vision.

The poet Robert Adamson once spoke to me of the 'calligraphy of the swamp' and that seemed right. The word cacophony came to mind as well, when a kookaburra started up, a solitary call, before being joined by dozens of them in a chorus that went on for several minutes.

I'd read up on the area in an attempt to understand what I would find when I got there. I'd also sought to understand the political context the Barmah Forest now exists in. I knew that this was Yorta Yorta land—had been for thousands of years. In response to a native title claim submitted by the Yorta Yorta in 1995 it was determined that the 'tide of history' had 'washed away' any real observance of traditional laws or customs by the applicants. Watery puns abound. An appeal was made to the Federal Court on the grounds that the judge had 'failed to give sufficient recognition to the capacity of traditional laws and customs to adapt to changed circumstances'.[12] The native title claim was still not recognised. In May 2004 the Victorian Government signed a co-operative management agreement, which gave the Yorta Yorta a say in the management of traditional country including the then Barmah State Forest. In 2010 the area became a national park.

In the presence of the river red gums you find yourself thinking about time differently. You wonder about the age of a particular tree, then suddenly you're contemplating what the landscape would have looked like a few million years ago.

---

12   Federal Court of Australia, *Members of the Yorta Yorta Aboriginal Community v Victoria & Ors*, [1998] FCA 1606 (December 18, 1998).

Six million years ago the spot I was standing on was a shallow sea. The group of eucalypt species that include the red gums evolved at least five million years ago. Two and a half million years ago a species akin to *Eucalyptus camaldulensis* had evolved, though even today there is pronounced variation between individual river red gums as well as between subspecies. These variations have resulted in significant historic misnomers and misrepresentations. It's worth mentioning here that the human fixation on categories leads to an illusion of clarity in the botanical world that is itself a misunderstanding. These blurring boundaries (and the resistance to recognising the blur) have serious implications in a time of human intervention in everything from the climate to the geographic spread of trees and their propagation. Such distinctions (or lack of) are more common in the popular press when it comes to fauna: polar bear or grizzly? Dog or dingo?

The time when the river red gum emerged, 2.5 million years ago, coincided with an earthquake that changed the geology of the area I was standing in, and also with a shift to a drier, cooler climate. Lakes evaporated and dunes formed. After this ebb there was flow again and as recently as 120,000 years ago Australia was a land of lakes. Over the millennia these ebbs and flows created a series of quite specific ecosystems, ones that could tolerate periods of both drought and inundation. The lakes reached their peak area around 32,000 years ago and, not coincidentally, the extensive river red gum forests in the mid-Murray region date back to this time. About 25,000 years ago, a displacement occurred along the

Cadell Fault, raising its eastern edge above the floodplain and transforming it into the Cadell Tilt. To my delight I saw this as I drove from Barmah towards the Cobb Highway: a ridge of the sand dunes from the ancient lakes that had been forced up as the land heaved. The Murray River flowed to the north and then the south attempting to get around the fault. The Goulburn River was dammed. As a result of all this activity, new water channels were drilled into the landscape, and existing rivers had to handle a much greater flow. An inland delta was created: the Barmah-Millewa wetlands we have today. The river gums of Barmah Forest have been dated, through pollen samples, to 3000 years ago, and the particular trees around me were (probably) up to 550 years old. River red gums are hard to age, though. Eucalypts don't develop annual rings, and they adjust their rate of growth to environmental conditions.

The river red gums have been managing, on their own, for millennia. But while the trees around me were certainly hardy, their environment has gone from being a robust system to a fragile one, from a self-regulating system to a dependent one. The Murray–Darling basin is now a regulated river system and the water released to maintain the wetlands must be negotiated with multiple (and successive) governments. This was something that became clearer to me as I walked along Broken Creek and past Rices Weir, where waterways were littered with skeleton trees; their banks lined by gums that appeared to totter on stilts, where their roots were exposed by erosion.

As the land rights ruling against the Yorta Yorta indicates, humans, like fauna and flora, are adjusting rapidly to an unprecedented rate of change. But governance structures are far less flexible than ecosystems, and those ecosystems are finding their capacity to manage change is blocked by human development and policy.

I emailed my brother, ecologist Dr Saul Cunningham, about these issues, in part because he has worked extensively on hybrid environments and, more specifically, because he's done research in Barmah Forest. My key question was this. Why don't we just allow environments to shift to a new normal and accept that losses are inevitable? Colloff phrases this more adeptly than I. 'Attempting to manage for static conditions makes little ecological sense if this does not reflect a natural process.'[13]

My brother told me that he thought the notion of normal, or even a 'new normal', was unproductive: the constant here was change.

Water flows, which drive everything, are essentially completely scheduled by humans. Water only flows down that river if the managers decide to let it. Some flows are essentially delivering water to users downstream (think of the river as a delivery pipe between the dams upstream and the farmers downstream). Some flows are allowed for environmental reasons. In the case of a manually

13   Colloff, p. 253.

operated system the question is no longer 'should wetlands be managed?' but 'how should they be managed?' What water should flow? When? And to what purpose?[14]

One challenge for ecologists is to map the way change was managed by river red gums in the past, and what that can teach us about managing the present, and the future. 'Nested within the landscape are the clues that tell how ecosystems have adapted to continuous change.'[15]

Another challenge is that these trees live for generations, whereas policies come and go in a decade. And those who care for the trees live only a fraction of the river red gum's lifetime. Two years after my visit to Barmah, a drought is ravaging New South Wales and Queensland. River red gums throughout the river system are dying in their thousands and fish are dying by the million. Former National Party leader Barnaby Joyce has been appointed as 'envoy for drought recovery' and suggested that water from the depleted Murray–Darling system be taken out of the rivers and passed on to the farmers. Governments should be asking if deforestation through New South Wales and Queensland is contributing to this drought and whether areas of Australia that (to quote Joyce himself) get the same amount of rainfall as parts of Saudi Arabia can sustain current models of farming. As far as I'm aware those questions are not being asked. There is some good news: by the end of

14   Private correspondence between the author and Dr Saul Cunningham, January 13, 2017.

15   Colloff, p. 253.

2018 a deal *had* been negotiated between state and federal governments to return up to 450 gigalitres to the environment, provided this doesn't have a negative socio-economic impact on river communities based on criteria agreed to by the states. However, at the time of writing an agreement on what is meant by 'negative socio-economic impact' has yet to be reached.

A sub-fossil that is probably *Eucalyptus camaldulensis*, removed from nineteen metres below the Yarra River, has been dated to 8780 years ago.[16] One reason these trees are considered sacred, indeed *feel* sacred, is that their presence traces the history of the elements, the lay of water above and below the ground. The roots of mature red gums go down ten metres, so a tree's condition can indicate how deep the ground water lies. The patterns of their growth can follow the traces left by the water of millennia past. Remnant forests mark swamps long drained and individual trees can outlive the existence of the waterways by centuries.

River red gums had various names bestowed on them by first settlers, including 'Yarra',[17] also the name of the river that runs from the Yarra Ranges to Port Phillip Bay. The river was first named Yarra Yarra by John Wedge, John Batman's private surveyor. Wedge believed Yarra Yarra was the name given to the river by the Kulin, though he later learned they'd been referring to the pattern and movement of water, not the river itself. Language was extrapolated from many

16   Colloff, p. 37.
17   Colloff, p. 21.

different clans. Georgiana McCrae, a painter and diarist who immigrated to Melbourne in 1841, translated the words *Yarra Yarra* as meaning 'flowing flowing', and the word *Yarrabing* as 'White Gum'.[18] The word for red gum in Yorta Yorta is quite different. *Biyala*.

The mashing of the word Yarra to mean several different things seems appropriate, given that the river red gum traces water, denotes it. The river and the red gums are, if you want to stretch the poetic point, as one. In a culture obsessed with classifications and difference I sometimes find this way of thinking—considering the not-difference between things— useful. To call a river a tree is, on the one hand, absurd, but it also draws attention to the interdependence, the relationships, that mean these two systems, forest and waterway, are a single ecosystem. The Yorta Yorta would argue that the interdependence is broader than that. A submission to the Victorian Environmental Assessment Council on Yorta Yorta connections with river red gum forests argued that there was a correlation between the loss of the Yorta Yorta's traditional lands and health problems within the community.[19]

River red gums give us pause. A consideration of their lifespan, and the time it took to create the right conditions for them to flourish, a consideration of what has occurred under and around their boughs, forces us to think more clearly about our place, its history, and our place in that history. These trees

---

18   *Yarra*, Kristin Otto, Text Publishing, 2005, p. 16.

19   Submission to Victorian Environmental Assessment Council (VEAC) on Yorta Yorta Connections with River Red Gum forest on public land in Study Region, Dr Wayne Atkinson, University of Melbourne, June 13, 2005.

survived the Central Desert's shift from a more temperate climate to today's fierce conditions, the ebbs and flows of the developing Murray–Darling basin. River red gums still manage to establish themselves along creeks that have been concreted, rerouted and repurposed. They will continue to trace historical water lines and find new ones, colonising riverbeds as they dry out, sending their roots down to the groundwater that still exists below. Our survival is linked to theirs. If the river red gum can find a way to regenerate successfully then maybe, just maybe, so can we.

COOLIBAH

COOLIBAH

(*Eucalyptus microtheca, E. coolabah*)

Once a jolly swagman camped by a billabong
Under the shade of a coolibah tree

BANJO PATERSON

ET'S be clear about this. The swagman under the coolibah (*Eucalyptus coolabah*) was not jolly. He stole a sheep, was caught by a squatter and rather than be captured by troopers for sheep stealing, he drowned himself. The coolibah, the provider of shade, stood sentinel: the only witness in an ongoing war between those who own sheep and those who would steal them.

Trees have witnessed a lot and, notwithstanding the way we abuse and exploit them, that gives them cultural cachet. In 1933 the Lone Pine (*Pinus brutia*), grown from a seed in a cone from a solitary pine on the Gallipoli Peninsula in Turkey, was planted at Melbourne's Shrine of Remembrance. That tree died in 2012 but was replaced by a descendant of the same pine. Today there are some two hundred memorial trees on the shrine's grounds. Many of our country towns have planted avenues of honour, tree-lined boulevards that commemorate the lives of local men and women who died in World War I. Ballarat in Victoria has the longest avenue (twenty-two kilometres and 3912 trees). The trees are usually deciduous—elms, oaks, poplars, plane trees—and the avenues are spectacular in autumn. A few more adventurous towns have planted avenues of flowering gums.

Alongside these official memorials, individuals have been carving their initials into trees for centuries. Basque shepherds carved pictures into aspens along the west coast of the United States, soldiers carved the initials of those they loved through the forests of France and Germany before going into battle. In Australia explorers carved their initials into trees as they walked and rode across the continent. In his great novel *Voss*, Patrick White captured the spirit in which they did so.

'Voss left his mark on the country,' he said. 'How?' asked Miss Trevelyan, cautiously. 'Well, the trees, of course. He was cutting his initials in the trees. He was a queer beggar, Voss. The blacks talk about him to this day. He is still there—that is the honest opinion of many of them—he is there in the country, and always will be.'

I've seen a faint S in one of John McDouall Stuart's trees, not far from Daly Waters, but there are several others known as Stuart trees, carved as he made his way, over several attempts, from the south to the north coast of Australia. Katoomba has the Explorers Tree, allegedly blazed by Blaxland, Lawson and Wentworth in 1813 after their successful crossing of the Blue Mountains. The tree, now a fenced-off stump by the Great Western Highway, is believed to be a fake carved early in the twentieth century to attract tourists to the area. The stump gets three stars on TripAdvisor and a couple of desultory comments.

Ludwig Leichhardt, the explorer upon whom White based Voss, blazed an ironwood tree (*Erythrophleum chlorostachys*) during his first expedition in 1844. That now sits, according to cultural and social anthropologist Richard Martin,[1] in a museum in Borroloola, 'amidst the flotsam and jetsam of the town's colonial history—weathered saddles, rusted stirrups, dingo traps, broken spectacles, glass bottles, moth-eaten uniforms, reproduced photographs, scraps of text'. Martin also writes of the Gregory Tree, a boab (*Adansonia gregorii*), which was named after the explorer who 'discovered it' near Timber Creek during his expedition of 1855–6. That tree is

---

1   '"Reading" the Leichhardt, Landsborough and Gregory Explorer Trees of Northern Australia', Richard J. Martin, *Cultural Studies Review*, vol. 19, no. 2, September 2013, http://epress.lib.uts.edu.au/journals/index.php/csrj/index pp. 216–36.

also a registered Aboriginal sacred site. In Burketown there is the Landsborough Tree, blazed by William Landsborough when he was searching for Robert O'Hara Burke and William John Wills. That tree was vandalised (burnt down) in 2002.

But the arborial star of the Burke and Wills show was, of course, the Dig Tree. In 1860, the Victorian Government sponsored an expedition to make the first south–north crossing of Australia to the Gulf of Carpentaria, a distance of 3,250 kilometres, led by Burke and Wills. Burke and the party reached Cooper Creek by December 1860. From there Burke and Wills travelled north with Charles Gray and John King while four men led by William Brahe were asked to wait with supplies for three months. They waited four.

At Cooper Creek there stood—and still stands—a spreading coolibah tree (*Eucalyptus microtheca*) now known as the Dig Tree, which stood patiently as instructions were cut into it. The first of these, carved by Brahe on April 21, 1861 before he abandoned hope and turned for home, read:

Dig
Under
3 FT NW

Wills saw the carvings only a few hours later, after he staggered into the camp with Burke and King. They were directions to find a buried trunk containing food supplies, but Burke became distressed upon seeing it, understanding, perhaps, that the tree was telling him he would soon be dead.

When the shattered group left the camp six days later, planning to walk west to Mount Hopeless (yes, really), Burke left a note in the buried trunk outlining their situation and plans. He decided not to inscribe a second message on the Dig Tree, so when Brahe returned to the camp on May 8 he saw no reason to dig and never received the message.

The Yandruwandha, whose land the Dig Tree stands on, were shocked by the incompetence of white explorers, but felt a sense of obligation to communicate the danger the men were in. Offers of help and friendship were extended but these offers were usually rebuffed. The explorers guzzled limited water reserves, fished and hunted indiscriminately and generally behaved like boorish intruders as tensions rose. Several Indigenous men, most notably a man known as Mr Shirt, were killed.

Towards the very end, in extremis, Burke, Wills and King did begin to observe the habits of the Yandruwandha and ate a porridge or bread made from the seeds of an aquatic fern called nardoo—filling, but insufficiently nutritious to sustain life in the long run. Some have argued that the nardoo actually poisoned them. Whatever the truth of this, hypothermia and other conditions such as beri-beri also contributed to their deaths.

There are multiple stories, some passed down by the Yandruwandha and some by the explorers who followed them in hope of finding members of the lost expedition. One such story concerns a fight between Wills and Burke after Burke rejected food from blackfellas. Another story is that Burke murdered Charles Gray; another that King murdered Burke. This may be literally true, or a moral story hinting that King would have been justified in killing Burke. King survived by living with the Yandruwandha for ten weeks. He fathered a child with a woman he knew as Carrawaw, who looked after him. Their descendants still live in the area today. A Yandruwandha man reported being haunted by Burke and Wills: 'What for whitefellow not send horses and grub?' He said their voices never left Cooper Creek.

Other than the word *Dig* the scars in the coolibah have begun to repair themselves: the history-eating coolibah. Trees like to eat things. There is a Moreton Bay fig in the Flagstaff Gardens that's eaten a metal possum guard. I've seen a plane tree in New York that's eaten a road sign. On Washington's Vashon Island in the Pacific Northwest there is a tree that's eaten a bicycle. Trees eat grenades, army helmets, entire houses.

The Dig Tree now has a heritage designation as both a cultural object and as remnant native vegetation. It grows by Cooper Creek, six kilometres from the Nappa Merrie homestead in a reserve owned by the Queensland Historical Society within a property owned by Stanbroke Pastoral Company. The Dig Tree is tourist attraction that attracts about thirty-five thousand tourists a year. (It gets four stars on TripAdvisor and many enthusiastic comments.) It is, the heritage listing notes, 'a wonderful looking tree'.

HISTORY ON UNTHINKING FEET

HISTORY ON UNTHINKING FEET

WANT to tell you about some walks I did, but first I'm going to tell you about a random thing that happened on one of my walks. After walking twenty kilometres or so, on a hot day in (I hoped, I imagined) William Buckley's footsteps, I went to say hello to a man who was the brother of the friend who'd picked me up at the end of my walk. My friend's brother was the 'guardian' of a 250-kilogram fur seal called Arcto and his job was to protect people from what was a large wild animal, not a cartoon character adept at balancing a ball on his nose. But Arcto needed protection as well—from selfie-takers who came too close, people who threw bottles, people who kicked sand in the seal's face. Arcto was seven years old and he'd visited Dromana Beach for three years in a row. He headed out to hunt in the evening, arriving back each morning around seven. The reason I had walked from Dromana to Sullivan's Bay then been returned to Dromana by the friend whose brother was Arcto's guardian was that I'd begun a project of walking around and outside Melbourne with the same purpose, or lack thereof, as I'd walked cities overseas.

In *Wanderlust* Rebecca Solnit writes that 'walking reshapes the world by mapping it, treading paths into it, encountering it; the way each act reflects and reinvents the culture in which it takes place'. This appealing idea suggests more conscious purpose than I ever felt. For me these excursions were a walking meditation. I set an intention, but didn't overthink it. I was finding my way home, I was staying with the trouble. I was thinking about the way my settler ancestors took up land in this country. Few of us have been here as long as veteran river red gums, my family only slightly longer than eucalypts have been growing in California. We're exotics, invasive, non-native.

I chased a history that shimmered, a force field of trauma, through the landscape of my homeland. On my first long walk, along the city's boundary lines, I found myself reciting the names of the significant roads, buildings and rivers under my breath. A silent chant. The names were a mix of the descriptive, nods to political power and royalty, the wives and daughters of political men, and echoes of the languages of the clans of the Kulin Nation: Nicholson, Princes, Lygon, Trin Warren Tam-boore, Westgate, Boundary, Moonee Ponds, Racecourse, Doutta Galla, Newmarket, Epsom, Langs, Maribyrnong, Coode, Fishermans Bend, Yarra, Lorimer, Kings Way, Dorcas, Shrine, St Kilda, High, Punt, Toorak (Turruk), Victoria. In this chant I heard the echoes of a history: violent and greedy, hopeful and desirous of a civil and cultured new world. On those walks I rediscovered the Carlton Gardens, Royal Park, the botanic gardens, magpies warbling, cockatoos screeching. I returned to my habit of putting a flower in Lady Gladys's hand every time I walked past the statue of her and her husband, Yorta Yorta man Sir Douglas Nicholls, in Parliament Gardens.

The Melbourne General Cemetery is a good spot to think about the history of this youthful city, one not yet two hundred years old. Before it was a graveyard it was a camp ground. Corroborees were danced here. Herein lies the grave of Boon Wurrung headman Derrimut, who died in 1864. Generous to a fault, he warned early settlers of an impending attack by tribesmen. His last (documented) words suggest that he regretted that: All the land 'along here Derrimut's once; no matter now, me soon tumble down...You have all this place, no good have children, no good have lubra, me tumble down and die very soon now.'[1] You'll find the graves of early

---

1   *First People*, Gary Presland, Museum Victoria Publishing, 2010, p. 91.

premiers and prime ministers. The miners' leader at Eureka Stockade, Peter Lalor, is buried here. A scan of the gravestones and monuments describes waves of immigration. The Scottish, English and Irish men who came first, and those who came not long after, with the gold rush of the early 1850s. Chinese, Jews, Italians, Greeks and Germans settled in Melbourne in significant numbers over the decades. The rise of fascism in the first half of the twentieth century, and World War II, drove even larger numbers to our shores.

My forebears were Scottish, my great-great-great-uncle, Ebenezer Syme, is buried in this cemetery—he died of tuberculosis in 1860, not so long after he arrived here, not long after buying a local newspaper called the *Age*. His brother David, my triple great-grandfather, lived longer, and became wealthier. He's buried in Kew, in an Egyptian-styled crypt. David Syme first came to Victoria looking for gold, after a couple of years in California where he'd also been searching for gold. After some prevarication he took over the paper Ebenezer had bought. He was a passionate protectionist, relentless, dour. He was a friend of Alfred Deakin, but argued against Federation. He saw that the selection of Crown lands before surveying was a means of breaking the squatters' monopoly and creating a farming population.

> Syme's undoubted power as a publicist encouraged the quicker development of things that became an accepted part of the fabric of Victoria than might otherwise have been the case. He encouraged small

farming, especially dairying, irrigation and water conservation, the opening-up of mallee lands, crédit foncier loans for farmers...[he] experimented with pasture improvement and drainage.[2]

Water. Everything comes back to water.

Between 1910 and 1914 Oswald Syme, David's youngest son, bought more than nine hundred acres at Mount Macedon, land that had been the pastoral runs Turitable and Wooling— Wooling meaning the 'nestling of many waters'. This land included a place once known as Bolobek Swamp, a rich source of food for the Wurundjeri people. Oswald, like his father, ran stock. He was also a chairman of the *Age* and the paper stayed in the Syme family until the Fairfax family arrived. They bought shares in the paper in 1972, and totally controlled it by 1983. The family lost control of Fairfax Media by 1993; and that company itself looks set to dissolve as I write, after a takeover by Channel 9.

Other ancestors also arrived in the mid-1800s. Some headed to Ballarat, some to Kalgoorlie. One great-great-great-grandfather, Alexander Wawn, was a weaver from Paisley, Scotland, who arrived in Victoria in 1841 and ended up in Brighton. Wawn was once spelt Waghen and the Waghens were Saxons which means that if you are really keen to stretch the point I'm descended from Vikings and other folk who lurked not far from Iceland. The Nicholls arrived in 1889 from

2   'Syme, George Alexander (1822–1894)', C. E. Sayers, *Australian Dictionary of Biography*, vol. 6, MUP, 1976.

England and settled in Ballarat. My great-grandfather on that side of the family, Percival, became editor of the *Ballarat Star*. His son, my grandfather Alan Nicholls, was also a journalist. He won the first Walkley awarded, back in 1956. That now graces my bookshelf. I could go on, but won't, as intrigued as I am by such snippets of family emails as 'your bohemian aunt shocked neighbours by having a gigantic nude painted on her back fence, and had many, many lovers…' That bohemian aunt once said, apparently, that 'all the Campbells suffered from melancholia'. Only my adoptive relatives (the Cunninghams), originally Irish, arrived in the twentieth century. They travelled by ferry to Glasgow, by train down to London then got on a steamer to Brisbane. That voyage took seven weeks through the Suez Canal, Sunda and Torres straits, stopping at Thursday Island, Cairns, Townsville and Rockhampton.

Two men buried at the Melbourne Cemetery who were particularly important to the opening up—aka theft—of lands in northern Australia were our old friends Robert O'Hara Burke and William John Wills. The block of granite that commemorates Burke and Wills stands in the centre of a very lovely grove of Port Jackson figs that, if the season is right, hang heavy with rusty brown fruit. The men died in June 1861 and their funeral was held in 1863, but the block of granite I looked at one wintery afternoon in 2016 was not inscribed until 1873. Squabbling attended the expedition's beginnings and haunted it till long after the men's demise.

A few hundred metres from the grave, across the way in Royal Park, not far from a magnificent stand of sugar gums, there's a monument to the expedition's departure. This was where a small group of us set off one afternoon, retracing the very modest first day of the Victorian Exploring Expedition to the Gulf of Carpentaria. That day was August 20, 1860 and the expedition then comprised six Irishmen, five Englishmen, four Indian and Afghani camel drivers, three Germans, an American, twenty-three horses, six wagons, twenty-six camels and twenty tonnes of baggage. They were carrying food to last two years and, among many other objects, a cedar-topped oak camp table and chairs, rockets, flags and a Chinese gong. I have read talk of a piano, but that strikes me as so absurd it must be a metaphor for the hubris that killed Burke and the six men he dragged down with him rather than a fact.

There were endless speeches before a crowd of some fifteen thousand and the expedition didn't leave till 4 p.m., so we didn't either and, like them, we walked, counter-intuitively, towards Royal Park's South Gate. We didn't get bogged as some in that expedition did; instead we walked briskly past what were once cattle yards near Park Drive. We turned north along Flemington Road, crossed Main's Bridge over the Moonee Ponds Creek, and wondered exactly where the Flemington Hotel (established 1848) used to be. These days Flemington Road feeds into the Tullamarine Freeway and is a dozen lanes wide, but then it was a rutted dirt track. We veered left along Mount Alexander Road, which existed back then, having been one of the main tracks taken by those who walked to the goldfields. We walked past the tram yards, negotiated the traffic lights at Moonee Ponds Junction and headed to the

Burke and Wills room at the Moonee Valley Bowling Club. We'd hoped for a counter tea, perhaps some camel steaks, but it was closed. The expedition camped in what is now known as Queen's Park and blazed a tree at the site to mark the spot. The tree died soon after but was maintained, albeit as a grim and ivy-covered stump, out of respect to the blaze and those who'd carved it until the council finally removed the stump in 1938. We stood and admired the memorial sculptures—camel silhouettes—and, after some sushi further down the road, got on a tram and headed home. We'd walked six kilometres, tops.

Indigenous people who lived along the expedition's route, especially those between Menindee and Cooper Creek, and Cooper Creek and Mount Hopeless, came to think of the camels on the expedition as emus because of the movement of their necks. Others decided they were bunyips. They became concerned about the litres of water the driven and thirsty animals would drink in a single session, wreaking havoc on their waterholes. They watched those camels variously die, escape and, in some cases, survive. (By 2013 there were six hundred thousand feral camels roaming central Australia, though not all of them were descendents of Burke and Wills' beasts.) All the horses taken on the expedition died. So did Ludwig Becker, who was left at Menindee with a splinter group when Burke decided a smaller group of men had more chance of making it to the northern coastline and back before the wet set in. The Royal Society had failed to provide Becker with the proper equipment and Burke, uninterested in scientific observations, had made him do a porter's work, which included loading and unloading the camels and carrying packs.

After that heavy labour Becker would sit up until late to complete his reports and sketches. Despite all this, he sent five full reports to the Royal Society of Victoria back in Exhibition Street, which was about five more than Burke sent. Becker made some seventy sketches, carried out meteorological observations and made notes on the Indigenous people he met along the way, including noting words of their songs. He was not paid for his efforts. His reports, including those warning the society that the expedition was failing, were ignored. He developed scurvy, dysentery and beri-beri. Ludwig Becker died on April 29 at Bulloo in the southwest corner of Queensland. An appalling end to the life of man who, when younger, had happily survived Victoria's goldfields armed only with a sketchbook and pet bat.

Becker pops up time and time again in the history books, a cheerful, talented and well-liked figure. He sent sketches from the goldfields in the early 1850s. He corresponded with John Gould on the matter of lyrebirds and his attempts to raise them as chicks. He sketched William Buckley not long before Buckley's death in 1856. Becker's miniatures, his landscape sketches and his Aboriginal drawings have been described by the Director of the National Museum of Australia, Andrew Sayers, as 'among the finest watercolours to be produced in Australia in the nineteenth century'.[3] This is no exaggeration.

---

3   daao.org.au/bio/ludwig-becker/biography/

His watercolours are highly atmospheric and even when bleak, have been achieved with the lightest touch. He drew an Indigenous man called Dick, who guided them for a while. He sketched Mr Shirt, who'd acted as a diplomat between his tribe and the men left at Bulloo Campa before being shot as Becker lay dying. He painted camels crossing the Terrick Terrick plains, ancient craters and the Mud-Desert near Desolation Camp. He sketched dogs eating human remains. The reservoir in the Mutawintji Ranges (called Mootwanji by Becker), as rendered by him, is as primal as a Mayan fertility figure. It made me think of Courbet's *Origin of the World*. His camels slide through moonlight, tropical plants glow silver white, a single meteor shoots through the sky.

Ludwig Becker and the subject of his severe portrait, William Buckley, were both open to what was extraordinary about this continent. Both died heavy of heart with the knowledge that wilful ignorance and cruelty would do their best to render the settler nation blind. William Buckley was not an explorer but an escaped convict. Nonetheless he succeeded in travelling far deeper into an understanding of the land in which he'd found himself than, possibly, any other white man in Australia's history. Buckley escaped from the Sullivan's Bay (Sorrento) colony with five other men back in 1803. One of his fellow convicts was shot at the outset; that left four to sprint around what is now known as Port Phillip Bay, known to the Boon Wurrung as Nairm, and known to the convicts as Port King.

They crossed the Yarra River at the Falls; two then headed

north in the hope of finding Sydney, and the remaining three, including Buckley, arrived at the You Yangs (Yawyangs), in two days by Buckley's own, possibly inaccurate, reckoning.[4] They kept on going to Swan Island, at what is now known as Queenscliff. At this point the two other convicts gave up and headed back east, out of the history books. Buckley kept going to Buckley's Cave, Point Lonsdale, mapping the land with his settler's feet, contributing to its naming. He lived in the cave awhile—maybe a year, maybe more—living off raw shellfish, slowly getting weaker. He began to consider returning to Sullivan's Bay as two of his fellow escapees had planned to, oblivious to the fact that the colony had been abandoned because of lack of water. As Buckley began the long trek back he found a spear driven into the ground at what is now known as Torquay. He pulled it out of what he did not recognise as a grave, to use as a walking stick. No fool, he knew there were natives around, but the spear marked him out as the spirit of Murrangurk and so Buckley was met with some ceremony by Wathaurong, at what is now the back of the Barwon Heads Golf Club. He stayed with these people on and off for thirty-two years.

Buckley's occasionally erratic behaviour was considered to be a result of the tricky business that goes with being a returned spirit. His survival has been attributed to skills that included diplomacy, a facility with language, and catching fish. He married. Once, maybe twice. He fathered a daughter.

4   *The Life and Adventures of William Buckley*, edited and introduced by Tim Flannery, Text Publishing, 2017 (original text first published in 1852 and written by John Morgan).

Then, around the time Melbourne was being settled, he saw Englishmen camped at Indented Head and approached them, intending to save them from a spearing by the more wary of his people. He'd lost his English but was handed a piece of bread. Buckley looked at the colonisers, he looked at the bread in his hand. The word came to him and he said it out loud. *Bread*.

> We brought him a piece of bread which he ate very heartily and told us immediately what it was. He also informed us that he has been above twenty years in the country, during which time he has been with the natives. Jim Gumm measured his height, which was 6ft. 7in. or 8in. He then told us that his name was William Buckley, having the following marks on his arm:– W.B. and marks like a crab, half-moon, and small man.[5]

And so they knew him as an Englishman, though Buckley could no longer tell what he was. Buckley's account of those years, given to two different journalists, was thought to be exaggerated, so extraordinary was the story he had to tell, but is now thought to be, give or take a literary flourish, close to the truth. His totem was the magpie and the 'small man' tattooed on his arm was in fact that small bird.

With each step we make / history on unthinking feet, writes Barry Hill in *Ghosting William Buckley* and that phrase sings to me. Unthinking. Unlearning. Unwriting. These are the words

---

5   William Todd's hand-written journal, July 6, 1835.

that make sense to me as I get older. Hill also suggests that Buckley's wife's totem was a swan, and that Buckley, a keen hunter of swans, forced her to eat swan once as punishment. This bothers me. Is it fiction? Is it true? Why would he have done that? Did he, in fact, do that? What is striking about Buckley's account of these years is what is not said. Was this vagueness, or respect for his Wathaurong family? Certainly he would have been in possession of secret business.

Those of us who walked from Sullivan's Cove to Dromana could not re-create what it might have been like to run from a camp, shots fired at your back, taking down one of your number, moving through land where no settlers had trodden, and speaking a language no white men had spoken. No, we were a group of ten, and the day was spring-warm but not as hot as it was in January 1803 when temperatures reached above forty degrees Celsius. We looked at settlers' graves. Moonah twisted and danced around us, filtering the light, as they had for thousands of years. There were once thirteen thousand hectares of coastal moonah and now there are 980, fragmented to such a degree that extinction is the likely result. If development doesn't degrade them, the rising seas will drown them. Coastal communities can shift in response to environmental change, but these responses unfurl over generations and the moonah are running out of time.

Did Buckley run through tea tree bower, golden tunnels in the evening light, and if he did was he in any state to register the beauty? Did his heart explode with unexpected

257

joy? Did he walk under the boughs of the very same trees we walked under? Moonah can live three hundred years, so it is possible. More likely he headed away from the coast as he cast around for a route to Sydney, a city he missed by the longest of shots. For how was a man to know where Sydney was? I imagine that he ran to what we now call Arthur's Seat, before looking across to the Yawyangs and allowing them to set his course.

We, in contrast, stuck to the coast. After several hours we came out of the moonah and coastal banksia forests and walked through the bay's shallow waters, trudged over the glistening white sands. The walk took us six hours and we were exhausted, minds washed clear. We'd laughed a lot. Swans skimmed, congregated, glid, snake-necked, broad-winged, red-beaked. I waded out to cool my feet and watched them. The great birds reminded me of the egrets at Alcatraz: their guttural honks, the expansiveness of their wings.

If Buckley had gone on the lam eight hundred years earlier than he did, he could have walked through the heart of the bay, then a grassy plain. In my imagination he is as powerful as a figure from the Old Testament, from the Dreaming, from the Koran, with his flowing beard, his moving across water, the spear taken from a grave, the spirit of a bird looking out for him, the moon carved into his arm, his taking of the bread offering, his unintended betrayal of the men and women who had been his people. Walking in the sun encourages grandiose thinking. I bring my mind back to the water lapping my feet. Sea-level rising in such a shallow bay means these beaches won't exist in a few decades. Our unthinking feet walk a vanishing beachscape, a porous and sandy place: the past, the future bleed. Our walk takes so long that the tide falls, then rises again as Nairm breathes in, then out.

367 COLLINS STREET

367 COLLINS STREET

(Falco peregrinus)

The falcon cannot hear the falconer

WILLIAM YEATS

ROOF gardens have sprung up through Melbourne's CBD in recent years. Some of them have planted trees and I'm keen to see how those trees meet the challenge of high winds and temperatures. But as well as thinking about trees on buildings, what about buildings *as* trees? For example, if you visit the building at 367 Collins Street,

Melbourne, you will find (and I quote) a 'landmark tower' that 'offers exceptional workspace across its 32 office levels. The double height entrance lobby creates a powerful first impression, and two levels of basement parking for 210 cars deliver ultimate convenience. A variety of bustling cafes on the ground and lower ground levels provide a "third space" for informal meetings.' This is all well and good but I can't for the life of me work out why they don't mention up front the best thing about the building: it has installed a camera that allows people to live-stream the peregrine falcons that nest up there.

Peregrines were close to extinction by the 1960s because the pesticide DDT impaired the females' ability to produce strong eggshells. In 1970 a team of scientists and falconers came together at Cornell University in upstate New York to bring back the birds, but so few of the falcons were left in the US they had to reintroduce them from other countries.

Their numbers in cities are now increasing: peregrine falcons do well in urban canyons. Tall buildings and bridges give them space and a perch for prey. They're 'weedy', which means that they travel well, thrive in a variety of new landscapes, reproduce quickly, and compete effectively against native species.[1] The most serious threat to their survival remains pesticides.

In 2017 viewers watched the live stream from 367 Collins Street as two chicks died after being fed pigeons covered in a toxic deterrent gel. The acid eats away at the skin of the feet and the toxin goes up the food chain. Adult falcons can

---

1   Quammen.

survive the poison but chicks rarely do. The gel is illegal in the CBD but the falcons hunt from up to ten kilometres from their nest so several councils need to revise their regulations if the problem is to be solved.

Peregrine falcons have been nesting at 367 Collins Street since 1991. It's a desirable spot because the building's southeast-facing windows trap the morning sun but not the afternoon heat. Falcons don't know how to build their own nests and instead occupy the nests of other birds on the ledges of buildings and cliffs. Before nesting boxes were installed, the breeding pairs—it hasn't always been the same two falcons—would lay their eggs in the gutter. That was hopeless—the eggs got cold and wet then failed to hatch.

In October 2018 four eggs were laid. Three hatched, and one chick survived to fledge. During the writing of the final draft of this manuscript, I would, upon awakening, go to 367collinsfalcons.com.au. When I first tuned into it I saw a peregrine, her back to the camera, her wings spread out to encompass the chicks she'd hatched. They were named over the following weeks by an (over?)enthusiastic Facebook group of about a thousand people that included me: Fluffy, Flappy and Flew.

The mother has yellow legs and yellow rings around her eyes. Her chest is speckled and her wings dappled grey and brown. Once her eggs hatched, I could see white fluff balls sticking their heads out from under her. Soon they were old enough to be left alone while she and her mate hunted for food. The results of the hunt, and the feeding of the chicks, was awesome to behold: the falcons would methodically rip up the pigeons they'd caught, occasionally chewing on the larger pieces to make them more manageable. The three chicks began to jostle in the hope of being given the best bits. One pushy gal always seemed to be fed first and got the most food. She shot up. A weaker chick often missed out on food altogether, slept more and didn't grow much—indeed never grew adult feathers at all. That was Fluffy.

With what seemed frightening rapidity, the two chicks that weren't the hapless Fluffy began to stomp up and down the ledge on muscular legs that looked like down-covered Elizabethan pantaloons. They strutted along their thirty-third-storey ledge, taking in the view across Melbourne. Soon they were flapping their stumpy wings, and soon those stumpy wings had feathers on them. Their down began to drop and the grey flight feathers came through. Occasionally you'd see all three of them piled together sleeping and forget the disparity for a moment; but over the days Fluffy faded, her eyelids came down, her head began to roll, and then she died. Her tiny body was sent off for an autopsy, which was how it was discovered she'd died of an illness caused by ingesting poisoned pigeons.

The very day that Fluffy died her parents herded the larger of the survivors to the ledge, and, almost literally pushed her off. Down she swooped, up she soared: Flew. The Facebook page began to fill up with videos people took of the parents giving flying lessons and the three falcons calling to each other above Melbourne's city buildings. The chick left behind worked hard. She flapped away, working on her wing muscles: Flappy. Her parents kept visiting and feeding her and we kept waiting for her to fledge. But then, like Fluffy, Flappy appeared to go blind. Her head began to roll about. She died, and it was hard to watch. Flappy had shown a real enthusiasm for life in the few weeks she had. On the nights after Flew left, Flappy took to standing on the ledge, sometimes with a parent, sometimes alone. She'd look out across Melbourne as the lights of the city came on at dusk, then flickered off at dawn; as the sun rose over the Dandenongs and the city came to life.

THE AGE OF LONELINESS

THE AGE OF LONELINESS

TRUSTEES Report, National Museum of Victoria, 1903:

On Saturday evening, 19th December last, the large
Indian Elephant, 'Ranee', died at the Zoological
Gardens, and both the skin and skeleton were
secured for the Museum. The whole of the

skinning and the rough fleshing of the bones was carried out under my personal, constant supervision at the Zoological Gardens; and I am pleased to have this opportunity to record the valuable assistance rendered by the Director, Mr D Le Souëf, and his staff during that time.[1]

Trustees Report, National Museum of Victoria, 1905:

The large Indian elephant 'Ranee', which died at the Zoological Gardens in December of last year, has been stuffed, and now occupies a special case in the main hall.[2]

Trustees Report, National Museum of Victoria, 1923:

The death of Mr T. F. Moore occurred very suddenly on the 2nd September last. Mr Moore was appointed to the position of Articulator and Osteologist on the 13th June, 1900, and during his 22 years' association with the Museum, the collections were enriched by numerous examples of his skill. One of the first examples of his work was the preparation and mounting of the skeleton of the large Indian elephant

---

1   Trustees Report 1905 (DOC/15/4134) National Museum of Victoria Zoological Department Report, Museums Victoria Archives, Vol/143; DOC/15/4700, p. 28.

2   Trustees Report 1905, p. 28.

'Ranee', which, together with the mounted skin, occupies a prominent position in the main hall.[3]

Ranee is no longer in the main hall of the museum. Her remains are in off-site storage, her skeleton disarticulated. I search for her in other ways and find a newspaper photograph of her, ghostly with age. She's looking square at the camera, dignified. Ranee was the first elephant in Australia. A gift from the King of Siam, she arrived in Melbourne from Calcutta Zoo on March 5, 1883. The trip lasted for some weeks, during which Ranee was tethered by chains to the deck, with a shed of sorts built over her head. During one particularly bad storm she is reported to have wrapped her trunk around the iron stanchions of her hut to support herself. After the ship docked in Port Melbourne she was taken to the police station at 113 Bay Street. These days 113 has dropped off the map, but there is a number 115 and the building itself is still there. It's a lawyer's office now. I know this because I walked in and asked the woman behind the front desk if it had once been the police station and she told me it had been. I didn't ask her if she knew how you'd fit an elephant through the narrow door.

Ranee was walked to Royal Park, where the zoo had been built in 1862. She was walked late at night, in the dark, so that there wouldn't be people panicking and horses stampeding. This was not an unreasonable concern. When Hanno the Elephant arrived in Italy in the winter of 1514 locals trampled

---

3   Trustees Report 1923 (DOC/15/4134), National Museum of Victoria Zoological
    Department Report, Museums Victoria Archives, Vol/143; DOC/15/4700, p. 17.

fields, crashed in roofs and tore through walls to see Pope Leo X's magnificent gift. Hanno died three years after he arrived in Rome aged seven, which is very young for an elephant. His remains were discovered under the Vatican in 1962. Elephants throughout history have been given as gifts, and throughout history have caused similar stirs.

I couldn't find a record of the exact route Ranee walked, so I walked the most obvious roads that existed back in 1883. I walked up Bay Street to City Road and Whiteman Street. I was stuck for a while at the Yarra, where I became fixated on how she would have crossed the river. Princes Bridge had been built by then, but it seemed a long way out of the way. There was a pedestrian bridge where Queens Bridge is now. I'd read something that suggested that bridge was a rope bridge, and assumed it wouldn't have been strong enough to carry her weight. When I called my mother to discuss this with her, she emailed me a series of paintings she'd found of animals being transported by raft. After we did the walk my fellow walker Kelly Gardiner did some digging around and found an engraving of Melbourne in 1880. Falls Bridge, as the earlier iteration of Queens Bridge was known back then, looked sturdy enough, so I suspect that is our answer. Then I walked along William Street, through the relative quiet of the Flagstaff Gardens—punctuated by calling birds and the occasional screech of possums—past the empty Victoria Market, which existed when Ranee walked slowly past, and even now looked much as it had for a century. I walked under the plane trees that line Royal Parade before heading into the darkness of Royal Park. The park was full of ghosts. Wind rustling sheoaks, the flapping of a fruit bat. The moon was bright, the sky was clear and the air cold.

In that half-light I got a glimpse of the otherness of the landscape and felt—or imagined that I felt—how it might have been for Ranee, just off a boat after a long voyage, walking through the darkness towards her servitude, none of her own kind with her, no possibility of shared language. And elephants do have language. Philosopher Don Ross's description of standing in a herd of elephants conveys this:

> The most peaceful group feels electric with communicative action. There's continuous eye contact, touching, trunk and ear movements to which others attend and respond. Elephants engage in low-frequency vocalisation, most of which you can't hear, but you can certainly see its effects.

He goes on to describe the multiple strategies elephants have for talking to each other, which sound (read) to me like a kind of purring. They generate vibrations in the ground and softer low-frequency vibrations in the air; sound emanates both from their trunks and their guts. They trumpet and use 'a range of standard trunk and head gestures' and formal ways of touching each other.[4] Ross goes on to argue that this capacity for language, this 'hypersociality' makes elephants (along with parrots, corvids and toothed whales) persons. Should bestow

---

4   'The Elephant as a Person', Don Ross, *Aeon*, October 24, 2018.

upon them, legally speaking, personhood.

The night a group of us did Ranee's Walk together, the streetlights dropped away as we got close to the zoo. We could hear the animals calling, smell them in the night air. The entrance looked much as it had for decades, give or take a few yarn-bombed palm trees. Ranee is reported to have walked the nine kilometres from the police station calmly until she saw the zoo, at which point she attempted to bolt. Was it the smell of other animals? Their calls? Did she imagine what lay ahead: public viewings six days a week, Monday to Saturday from 11 a.m. until 12 midday and from 2 p.m. till 4.00 p.m. in the charge of her keeper? The society's minute book for March 19, 1883 records that she was 'gentle and in good health' and that she was undertaking training so she could give people rides, which, it was reckoned, she'd be able to do after two weeks. The impetus was pragmatic. The *Age* reported in early 1890 how much the fast-growing 'patient monster' ate; but also that, as a favourite with children, 'it' earned its own living. Ranee's upkeep amounted to £150 per annum; average takings for rides round the enclosure were £170.

The thing I kept asking myself, that felt most pressing, was this: was she lonely?

Lonely. The head of biology at Buenos Aires Zoo, Adrian Sestelo, has argued that it is inappropriate to compare an animal's responses to a human's. 'When you don't know the biology of a species, to unjustifiably claim it suffers abuse, is stressed or depressed, is to make one of man's most common mistakes, which is to humanise animal behaviour.' At the time of that statement Sestelo was weighing into a debate about one particular animal, Sandra the orangutan. Sandra had been held in a cage with iron bars and had nowhere to hide. She was distressed by being constantly on display and used to (still does) cover her head with a piece of cardboard or a cloth. She was the only orangutan at the Buenos Aires Zoo.

I too think anthropomorphism can lead to false sentimentality, but it is impossible to live closely with any animal, to become intimate with one, and not see that it has a rich emotional life. I could, but won't, throw any amounts of research at you, tell you of elephants who weep, mourn, honour their dead; of lions remembering those who freed them from captivity; gorillas who are intimate with their human family members; dolphins who've fallen in love and even tried to have sex with humans; of my arthritic old cat. It's a miracle I've managed to write an entire book and got this far without mentioning my cat Wilson who, in old age, seems to be kept alive by the love and friendship that exists between him and Virginia and me, his human comrades.

The Melbourne Zoo has evolved since Ranee's time, but she haunts me when I walk Royal Park, as I do most weeks. In its earliest days, housed in the Botanic Gardens, the zoo was an acclimatisation zoo and accommodated rabbits, foxes, kangaroos and starlings. After it moved to Royal Park the zoo became interested in a more exotic range of creatures. They also wanted, indeed needed, to charge entrance fees, and Ranee was the star attraction. During her twenty-one-year residence she contributed five per cent of the zoo's annual income.

In 1888 the zoo set up an ethnographic village as a part of their fiftieth birthday celebrations. Woiwurrung and Boon Wurrung living in Coranderrk, near Healesville, were brought back to their traditional lands. Weapons were arranged carefully around them. They were asked to throw boomerangs while onlookers stood around and watched. Stuffed animals added to the atmosphere. The Royal Melbourne Zoo is not the only zoo with such tales to tell, of course. In 1906, the Bronx Zoo kept a Congolese pygmy named Ota Benga in the monkey house after he'd been kidnapped by slavers. Benga wore modern clothes and entertained the crowd by shooting a bow and arrow at a target. He made friends with one of the orangutans, which the crowd found extremely amusing. An African-American clergyman, the Reverend James H. Gordon, took exception to this and successfully lobbied for Ota's release. There was a period when Benga was allowed to roam the grounds of the zoo but he became violent, and so he was moved out altogether. Benga shot himself in the heart after the outbreak of World War I prevented his return to Africa. 'It was a mistake,' said John Calvelli, senior vice-president for public affairs of the Wildlife Conservation Society, which owns and runs the zoo, in 2006. 'When you reflect on it, you realise that it was a moment in time. You have to look at the time in which it happened, and you try to understand why this would occur.'[5]

Philosopher Peter Singer has described the history of human moral progress as an expansion of the circle of beings we regard as persons, which makes sense to me. In 2012 People

---

5   'The Scandal at the Zoo', Mitch Keller, *New York Times*, August 6, 2006.

for the Ethical Treatment of Animals (PETA) was unsuccessful in invoking the US Constitution's 13th Amendment abolishing slavery and involuntary servitude to gain freedom for orcas in captivity. In 2013 the Nonhuman Rights Project initiated three legal claims on behalf of four chimpanzees in New York State. Initially rejected, the cases moved into a series of appeals that continue some five years later. In late 2014 Sandra the orangutan was declared a 'non-human person'. She was finally to be taken off display. 'The ruling was historic,' according to Andrés Gil Dominguez of the Association of Professional Lawyers for Animal Rights in Argentina, 'because before a nonhuman primate like Sandra was considered an object and therefore there was no dispute about its captivity.'

This story has no happy ending, though. A new home was never found for Sandra and she is too institutionalised to survive in the wild. Even if she weren't, there is barely enough wilderness to sustain her. Orangutan are a critically endangered species in part because deforestation, the production of palm oil, and the endless bushfires that have destroyed their habitat. The Indonesian government recently released figures suggesting the populations are bouncing back dramatically, but scientists have refuted those figures—it is not biologically possible for orangutan to breed at the rate suggested and there is no evidence of this increased population. On the contrary, many believe the orangutan will be extinct in the wild within a decade.

This leaves zoos with a dilemma. Outgoing director of the Melbourne Zoo Kevin Tanner recently commented that zoos 'should only be in existence if they want to save animals in the wild'. [6] But he also acknowledged that the world outside seemed to be getting worse: species loss, habitat destruction and climate change all increasing at a rapid pace.

While Sandra's enclosure has been improved since the court decisions, she still doesn't have much space. Judge Elena Liberatori, the judge who made the ruling on Sandra's personhood and has been in charge of overseeing improvements for her, managed to convince a ferry company to donate some ropes for her to play with. 'Her natural habitat is missing, and I think she'll never have it,' Liberatori said. 'I wish she had soil, grass, plants. They have a tree now. It was one of the improvements, but it's just some wood, not a real tree.'

Ranee died on December 18, 1904 of 'a very large accumulation of biliary calculi, weighing over 100 lbs., in the liver, that organ having been almost completely destroyed. The accumulation must have been going on for years…' In her final years she was not as 'gentle' as she once had been. In particular, she wouldn't let anyone near her mouth, and after she died it was discovered that one of her molars had grown thirteen centimetres longer than it should have, causing her a lot of pain. But she was, in the end, not totally alone. She became attached to one of her keepers and when he lay on the grass sleeping or resting she'd stand over him and wave flies from his face with her trunk. If people tried to approach him when he was resting she'd become angry and force the visitors back.

<hr />

6   'Leaving Time at the Zoo', Liam Mannix, *Age*, December 16, 2018.

At the same time I was researching Ranee's life—not long after the death of my dad, John—Peter, my biological father, went into care. From the moment of his diagnosis, Parkinson's disease, what he feared most was losing cognitive function. After many years of living with the illness, that loss became undeniable. Through 2017 I visited him most weeks. He was deeply distressed by his dementia, but what I found more alarming, to be honest, was his body's constant restlessness. He lurched up and raced off. Some days he couldn't stop walking. I'd find myself chasing him down corridors at a trot and when I finally caught and grabbed him bodily—at his request—he kept on moving, ramming the walking frame into me and the furniture around him. He couldn't turn himself off. He'd lose balance and fall. If I was in the room I'd try and catch him but, let's face it, I'm not young anymore. My back is not great and I do not do the various exercises for it that I should do. I struggled, physically I mean, to cope with the situation. On one visit my father just looked at me, then put his head in his hands and cried. But on other days he was cheerful and I walked him around in a wheelchair and he enjoyed the garden. There was a sculpted birdbath with bronze parrots, which he liked, as did I. He'd get up from his chair when we passed it, to pat the parrots on their shiny heads. One day he seemed to forget I was pushing his chair and said to the friend we were walking with, 'I thought Sophie had disappeared but I see her more now.' And it was true I was visiting him more in The Home than I did in his home. On another day, he told people that I was dead.

Rage hit me, from time to time, like a gale-force gust. Knocked me sideways. These men who came into my life, then left it to build other families. These men who expected me to love them unconditionally, despite the mess of life and bad behaviour (theirs, mine). These men who I nonetheless tried to offer care to as they died, and who did their best to love me.

One day I wheeled Peter under an oak tree and stopped to take a picture of it for @sophtreeofday. I told him I was planning to lead a walk I called Ranee's Walk, in honour of an elephant. I didn't tell him that elephants reminded me of trees, particularly old river gums when they silver to the colour of an elephant's hide. There are so many things that I never took the chance to tell my father about me, his only daughter, the random collection of thoughts I have most days, thoughts that I have attempted to bring together here, in this book. Likewise there are so many things he never told me. I wish he'd told me the kinds of things he mentioned that afternoon, one of the last I spent with him.

Things like this: when he was a small boy he'd ridden Betty, the elephant at the Royal Melbourne Zoo. Betty was not Ranee's successor—that was Queenie, who arrived at the zoo in 1902. Queenie gave rides for forty years to up to five hundred children and parents each day, walking an estimated 165,000 kilometres around and around the same enclosure. Hard surfaces are painful for elephants' sensitive feet. Many of them die of arthritis after years of pounding bitumen, and these days foot and joint problems are regarded as the most important health issue for captive elephants. Melbourne's bull elephant

Bong Su was euthanised in late 2017, after forty years at the zoo, when the pain from his arthritis became unmanageable. Peter Stroud, former curator at Melbourne Zoo and director of Werribee Zoo, wrote at the time:

> I have come to the realisation that zoos are no place for elephants. It is long overdue for Australian zoos to courageously confront the substandard conditions their elephants endure and look for better ways to provide for them. Bong Su is dead. Not because he reached old age, but because he was broken by cramped and impoverished zoo conditions and a terrible inability, through much of his life, to meet his true needs.[7]

At least Bong Su was loved by those who cared for him. Queenie not so much, though the general public adored her. Queenie's keeper was a man called Wilfred Lawson. Kenneth Brown, Lawson's nephew, remembers riding on Queenie's head as a schoolboy. 'I would help Uncle wash her down,' Brown says. 'It was a big job to wash her down, wipe her all over and dry her.' She was given a lot of rubbish to eat by children, and Brown cleaned out her mouth. He says she was very gentle and would turn over for them during her bath. But he also said that Lawson often hit Queenie with a stick. 'I didn't like my uncle hitting her,' Brown has said. 'He used to belt her to get past the monkeys.'

---

7   'Bong Su is dead, broken by cramped and impoverished zoo conditions', Peter Stroud, *Sydney Morning Herald*, October 13, 2017.

Queenie trampled Lawson to death in 1944.

'My dad believed it was deliberate, because Mr Lawson was pretty rough with her,' Joyce Hamilton, the daughter of a second elephant keeper, Adolphus Stanley, told a journalist sixty years after the event. She remembered hearing the news and being worried that it was her dad who had died. When she rushed home she found him sitting in his chair, alive and well. Stanley had looked after Queenie for a month while Lawson was on holidays and they'd got on well. Hamilton believed that after a month of her father's care Queenie cracked once Lawson returned from holidays and resumed his job.[8]

Adolphus Stanley considered Queenie 'the loveliest animal in the zoo'. It was he who shot her in 1945. The zoo said this was because of food shortages but it's hard not to imagine that her killing of Lawson and the consequent impact on her use as an income earner were also factors. Betty, the elephant Peter rode, replaced Queenie in 1939, along with an elephant calf called Peggy. That pleases me—that Betty had a friend. Peggy and Betty generated a lot of income for the zoo, but elephant rides were stopped in 1962 on the grounds that they were cruel.

I wondered why Stanley had agreed to shoot Queenie if it was true that he'd cared for her, but then read he'd done so to ensure her death was quick. This is something of a relief if you've read George Orwell's account of shooting an elephant, which Orwell himself equated with murder.

After three shots, wrote Orwell, the bull was not dead.

---

8   All quotes from Kenneth Brown and Joyce Hamilton come from 'Queenie's Last Ride', Mary O'Brien, *Age*, August 9, 2006.

He was breathing very rhythmically with long rattling gasps, his great mound of a side painfully rising and falling. His mouth was wide open—I could see far down into caverns of pale pink throat. I waited a long time for him to die, but his breathing did not weaken. Finally I fired my two remaining shots into the spot where I thought his heart must be. The thick blood welled out of him like red velvet, but still he did not die. His body did not even jerk when the shots hit him, the tortured breathing continued without a pause. He was dying, very slowly and in great agony, but in some world remote from me where not even a bullet could damage him further. I felt that I had got to put an end to that dreadful noise. It seemed dreadful to see the great beast lying there, powerless to move and yet powerless to die, and not even to be able to finish him. I sent back for my small rifle and poured shot after shot into his heart and down his throat. They seemed to make no impression. The tortured gasps continued as steadily as the ticking of a clock. In the end I could not stand it any longer and went away. I heard later that it took him half an hour to die.[9]

I've seen elephants in the wild, most notably in Sri Lanka, where I saw a mother feeding her baby. I've visited an elephant orphanage and watched elephants washing each other, and

---

9 'Shooting an Elephant', George Orwell, 1936.

being washed by their keepers, in a broad river that ran through the estate; seen calves being fed from the bottle. But such positive sightings are rare. On the trip to Los Angeles where I tracked, or imagined that I tracked, P-22, I visited the LA zoo's 'revamped' elephant enclosure. It was appalling. They had nowhere to get away from the public gaze. They were always being looked at and they clearly hated it: stood with their backs to us, faces pushed into the wall, rocking. I stopped looking. When I got back to our accommodation I took to the internet and found that those elephants were named Billy, who was thirty-two, and Tina and Jewel, who were in their early fifties. In 2012 a Los Angeles Superior Court judge ordered the zoo to exercise the three Asian elephants at least two hours a day on soil rather than concrete to reduce the impact on their legs and pads. The injunction also banned the use of electric shocks, and a barbed stick known as a bull hook. In May 2017 the court's ruling on the elephants' behalf was overturned.

I read a lot about elephants to prepare for Ranee's Walk, and subsequently to write this essay, including an essay that described the last surviving matriarch of her herd heading to a clifftop every night to feel the waves pound on the rocks then reverberate up through the rock and into her, making her feel less alone. I found this intensely distressing and had to put the essay down. My nerve began to fail me. Having undertaken to bear witness to what humans are doing to this planet, to all that lives upon it, I found I was beginning to look away. To read less about what was happening in the world in general, to elephants (and trees) in particular.

286

When I was flying across America in early 2018 I read a book that spoke about the notion of narrative fallacy, which means, in effect, trying to neaten things with hindsight, or to create a logical discourse through the inclusion of incidental details that are not, in fact, related. I found myself thinking about this a lot on that flight, because I was writing these essays, and because I am interested in finding patterns in seemingly random events, and then a few hours after I got off the plane I found out that Peter had died. A few months later, when a friend read a draft of this essay she commented, 'It's really about repressed grief, isn't it?' And I was horrified. Not because she was wrong, but because I don't want to suggest that the natural death of a parent is in any way akin to the grief that we may soon live in a world where there will be no elephants left in the wild.

Loss, and grief, can feel like many strands or like one large knot. The emotion does not necessarily make you cry, or even feel sad, but leads to a certain unravelling of self as that knot comes undone. Going about your day as you once did is difficult. The very idea of self feels like a narrative fallacy, the kind of fallacy that makes you consider Ranee's disarticulated skeleton as a metaphor, before you realise using her like that makes you feel physically ill. I don't want to make Ranee's story more meaningful by generating a shape to her life that is pleasing. I do not want to give in to the siren song of a resolved narrative. One that makes sense of what humans are doing to this planet, or what the passage of time does to us.

James Bradley writes of this complicated compression of grief in a beautiful essay about the recent loss of his father in the midst of the unfolding climate catastrophe.

> Grief teaches us that time is plastic. A lifetime is an ocean and an instant. It does not matter whether something happened a week ago, a year ago, a decade ago: all loss is now. Grief does not stop, or disappear. It suffuses, inhabits us. The dead are both gone and never gone, living absences we bear with us. Perhaps something similar is true of extinction. What is lost remains with us, felt in its unpresence.[10]

When Ranee died there were a few million African elephants and about 100,000 Asian elephants. Today, there are an estimated 450,000–700,000 African elephants left and about a third the number of wild Asian elephants. Elephants weep for the loss of their kin, and we humans should be weeping for them too. But not just weeping. We should also be fighting for their survival.

Before the flight across America where I'd been meditating on the idea of narrative fallacy, I'd been in Mexico. I was meeting friends on Isla Mujeres, not far off the coast of Cancun. I caught a ferry and then a taxi, and put my suitcases down in my room before walking through a grove of coconut palms to the beach. I'd been thinking about that swim for a long

---

10   Bradley, 2018.

time. When I got to the peerless blue-green ocean I found that the hotel had roped off a small section of water and we were allowed to paddle there, or stand there with cocktail in hand, but not allowed to swim out into the ocean itself. I don't know if the problem was the boats, or rips, or pollution. I stood with the warm water lapping my knees, surrounded by the crowds, watching people taking selfies and remembered a scene from the book, or perhaps the film, of Kurt Vonnegut's *Slaughterhouse Five* in which humans live in a zoo.

A night or so after standing in that water fighting off claustrophobia I was told Peter's health had taken a dramatic dive and that he might live only a few hours. I returned to Los Angeles the next day but did not cancel my plans, which were to fly to Indianapolis, Indiana, then drive to Bloomington. Flying home to watch another father die seemed beyond me. Not again: that is what I kept thinking. Not again. It was not the death itself I couldn't stand, but the pattern. Waiting in LAX as my fathers died, first one, then the other; sitting in darkness for fourteen hours, a sardine in a can, thinking of how things might have been different.

Four hours after I arrived in Bloomington, around midnight, I got the call to tell me that Peter was dead. I lay in a strange bed in a strange house hundreds of miles from the sea, and listened to the heating go on and off through the length of that long freezing night. I thought of the first time I said goodbye to him. We were standing in a room in an apartment in Boston in 1968. I was four years old. I was trying to understand why he wasn't returning to Australia with us, his family. And now here I was in another anonymous apartment in America, but this time Peter wasn't in the room telling me how much he loved me.

I found it hard to sleep over the next few weeks. Back in Melbourne, if I couldn't sleep I would close my eyes and list the names of AFL teams. Or (really!) imagine the movement of animals throughout the city and throughout history: the herding of sheep and cattle at night, skies filled with birds, Ranee's walk, sheep dogs mustering at the Royal Melbourne Show, horses running the track at Flemington. All manner of creatures still inhabit my city. Fruit bats fly overhead, seagulls circle the lights of the MCG; and some summer nights the sound of cicadas still fills the air. Snakes live along the riverbeds and creek beds, tiger snakes can be found in the CBD. Possums wreak havoc on our gardens. Around the wharves and wastelands of Port Melbourne as many as twenty foxes prowl every square kilometre.

But I couldn't project myself into such a world here in Bloomington. Double glazing on the windows meant that the heating was often the only sound I heard at night, until summer arrived and air con ramped up throughout the neighbourhood. Instead I played sounds on my iPhone: rain, a breeze, waves breaking on a beach. And then, if I was awake—I often was—I took to opening the windows around dawn so I could hear the sound of the birds or, failing that, the sounds of rain, of building works, of frat-house parties. Anything. Anything other than the sound of nothing at all.

And one day I took myself off to a conference on Kurt

Vonnegut, which was weird, as he'd been on my mind since I'd stood in the ocean imagining I was in a zoo, and also weird because Peter had written about him over the years. Vonnegut was a Hoosier, and that is one reason why Indiana University was having a conference about his work. I was at Indiana University to work on a novel, so Vonnegut was really a distraction, and now I find I can't remember much detail of the conference at all, except for the statement about trauma and the opening words of a speech he gave in Indiana some time in 2004. I don't know what the speech was meant to be about, or was going to be about, or where or why he gave it. I can only remember his opening line: *I'm sorry. I'm sorry. I'm sorry.* Another speaker spoke of Vonnegut's inability to write about the trauma either of his mother's sudden death, or of the firebombing of Dresden, which he'd witnessed soon after her death, in a direct fashion. Is that why Orwell couldn't stay with the elephant he was forced to kill, I wondered? Why my gaze, my oath to bear witness, was wavering? Why I, *we*, keep living in air conditioned houses and eating meat and voting in elections and being outraged on social media and going about our day-to-day business when it is the breadth of a deeper and wider timespan: the lifespan of an elephant, of a father, of a tree, of the glaciers and icecaps, of bedrock, we must start to truly comprehend?

MOUNTAIN ASH

Another glider!

Leadbeaters

Eucalyptus Regnons →

Glider

← 'Normal' gum

MOUNTAIN ASH

(Eucalyptus regnans)

ANTHROPOMORPHISING particularly significant trees can be useful. I mean useful in the strategic sense, to advance the political action required if trees are to survive the anthropocene in a meaningful way. But there is more to it than that. I'm also responding to my genuine sense, when spending time among trees, that trees have personality. That they are, in a way, sentient. Sure, that 'personality' is sculpted by weather, soil and light, and by the creatures that live in and around it. But it doesn't mean that feeling isn't worth attending to.

Such enthusiasms make people uncomfortable. 'Look, trees are networkers,' cautions British scientist Richard Fortey. 'They do communicate in their own way. What worries me is that people find this so appealing that they immediately leap to faulty conclusions. Namely, that trees are sentient beings like us.'[1]

I see it this way: trees need strategic thinking in these difficult times, and also they need friends. It was in the spirit of both friendship and activism that I went to visit the largest tree in Victoria. Her name is Ada and she's a mountain ash, one of the tallest flowering plants on earth. She is a queen, an empress—a goddess—of trees. To find her I drove through patches of clearfelled forest, past the shattered, dismembered corpses of trees lying in the mud. You can see these areas from a distance, patches of harsh light that contrast with the filtered light of their forested surrounds. Whatever your view on logging, seeing clearfelling like this is to see a wounded landscape—and this particular wound was still bleeding.

I walked for a couple of kilometres through myrtle beech rainforest to visit her. I walked along the banks of clear creeks past stands of tall fern trees. It was a peaceful walk, through what felt like an older landscape, which I suppose it

---

1 Quoted in 'Do trees talk to each other', Richard Grant, *Smithsonian Magazine*, March 2018.

is. Cool temperate rainforest in Victoria is rare, a remnant of when Australia was a part of Gondwanaland, more than 130 million years ago. Although relatively small in overall size, these rainforests are the home to thirty per cent of all Victoria's rare or threatened flora species. The tiny patches left huddle in south-facing gullies in fertile and high rainfall areas. They are an irreplaceable part of the Victorian natural landscape.

The walk took a bit less than an hour. The dense canopy, the leaden clouds, the narrowness of the gully lent the air a soothing greenish glow. As I emerged into a slightly dryer, more open landscape I began to see mountain ash around me. By the time I approached Ada I was feeling all the reverence due a tree of her station.

I stood before her; leaned forward, tentative, as if to touch her, then spread my arms out to get some perspective on her girth. I'm sure if you had been an outsider watching me you'd have thought I was about to embrace her. I craned my head back and tried to see into her crown. Ada is seventy-five metres in height, though some mountain ash reach a hundred metres. Long strands of bark drape from her like a cloak. Her crown is ragged, torn about by storms. She's some four hundred years old, plump with carbon, and her girth is some fifteen metres. She provides shelter for more than forty species of vertebrates and innumerable more invertebrates.

Large and long-lived animals seem to be among the creatures most vulnerable to decline and possible extinction. Apex predators, for example. Or whales. Large and long-lived trees are similarly vulnerable. Entire papers have been written

297

on how you define large, or long-lived. I'm skipping that, going straight to why these trees are so important, which is simply that if we lose all our old-growth forests the implications are devastating. These trees are not simply larger versions of their younger selves. Up to thirty per cent of our mammals rely on cavities found only in trees that are hundreds of years old. Some marsupials and birds get so attached to the particular tree they live in that they will stay in the place the tree existed before it was logged, much as humans continue to live next to the remains of their house after a disaster strikes. Old trees' crowns stand high above the forest and contribute less fuel to bushfires than middle-aged and young trees. When large old mountain ash fall, they decompose over time. The work of large old trees continues for decades or even centuries after their death. Their reign is long.

When I read Rebecca Giggs on whale fall I was struck by the similarity between trees and whales. Both have a capacity to feed an ecosystem for years and decades *after* they have died: 'Their massive bodies eventually sink, and simultaneously decay as they sink,' until finally the whale:

> drops, falls quickly to the sea floor, into the plush cemetery of the worms. Gusts of billowing silt roll away. The mantle of the whale's pulpier parts settles over it. Marine snow (anonymous matter, ground to a salt in the lighter layers of the sea) beats down ceaselessly. Rat-tails, devouring snails and more polychaetes appear. The bones are stripped and then

fluff up with silver-white bacteria, so that it appears as if the skeleton is draped in metres of downy towelling. Years may pass, decades even, before there is nothing left except a dent that holds the dark darker.[2]

Some trees are the equivalent of a city, so many millions do they support; such massive infrastructure do they provide. Others are more like towns; some are no more than a beach shack. The word *tree*, I'm starting to realise, is pretty vague. A creature that clones itself can be a tree, a creature with mobile sperm can be a tree, trees can change sex, trees can be hybrids, trees can kill humans (though more often they are their saviours), trees are both welcome and reviled. Some can live alone but some, like mountain ash, are happier living together. Don't believe me, a mere tree hugger: believe the statistics. Trees transplanted to city streets might be lucky to live twenty or so years, forest trees can last millennia. Size is important in a tree and older trees have this advantage also. They stand taller. Their cavities are deeper. Their buttress roots are higher and more complex. Micro-climates form around them. They push nutrients down into the soil. They hold the forest floor together. They make a forest less vulnerable to bushfire. A forest without large old trees is like a city without enough food, water, housing or clean air.

Mountain ash forests are among the most carbon-heavy forests in the world and that's a good thing, unless you're cutting them down. Which we are. Mountain ash constitute

2   'Whale Fall', Rebecca Giggs, *The Best Australian Essays 2016*, Black Inc., 2016.

one of the largest pieces of infrastructure in Victoria's crucial wet-forest ecosystem, and are one of the least protected from logging. Only 1.16 per cent of the mountain ash estate is now old growth. That's down from about sixty per cent. What we are left with is large old trees, known as singleton trees—yes, just like in Bridget Jones—in otherwise young forests. Queen Ada is a singleton. If she and others like her are not protected the results will be catastrophic.

It's tricky to manage old trees over long lives—'in many old-growth forests, the history of industrial logging is many centuries shorter than the lifespans of the trees being harvested'—but that is all by the by at this point. If changes to logging practices aren't introduced immediately the mountain ash ecosystem will collapse, dragging the other plant species and mammals they support with them, possibly some humans as well. The forest 'generates most of the water for the ~4.5 million people in Melbourne, stores large amounts of biomass carbon, and supports timber, pulpwood and tourism industries'.[3]

Australia has an appalling record of seeming disregard for its natural worth: its reefs, trees, rivers and more. Back in the 1920s 'the American Museum of Natural History had been so concerned about the ferocious removal of Australian trees that it had made collecting from the country one of its highest priorities'.[4] Little has changed. You can't simply heritage-list the large old trees and clear everything else. In any case the

---

3   'Hidden collapse is driven by fire and logging in a sociological forest ecosystem', David B. Lindenmayer and Chloe Sato, *PNAS*, vol. 115, May 15, 2018.

4   Hay, p. 147.

few legislative protections for forests in place (which include, for example, banning clearing along rivers and creeks) are routinely ignored. At the end of 2018 it was reported that 'trees making up some of Victoria's most endangered ecosystems are being felled and turned into building products, paper or woodchips by VicForests, which are then sold in retailers such as Bunnings and Officeworks'.[5]

Less than ten per cent of Australia's pre-settlement forests remain. Among these is a stand of mountain ash in Tasmania known as the Valley of the Giants. The former Greens senator Bob Brown has drawn parallels between the destruction of these trees and the Taliban blowing up the Bamiyan Buddhas in Afghanistan. Both are acts of desecration. There is money to be made in harvesting old-growth timber, sure, and there are jobs in it. But much as Japan's whaling industry exaggerates their citizens' cultural fervour for eating whale meat, logging advocates exaggerate both the market for old-growth timber and the quality of that timber: the Wilderness Society has argued that as much as sixty per cent of old growth trees are unusable.[6] In what universe would a reasonable person think it was okay to cut down an 800-year-old tree and reduce it to a few hundred dollars' worth of woodchips? Ours, apparently.

Richard Flanagan's essay 'Out of Control', written a decade ago, paints an extraordinary portrait of corruption, political will and devastation in Tasmania's Styx Valley:

5   'Australia's endangered forests are being "stolen" and sold in hardware and office stores', Michael Slezak and Penny Timms, *ABC News*, November 21, 2018.

6   'Old-growth trees to be "woodchipped, wasted" under specialty timber access plan', Rhiannon Shine, *ABC News*, August 4, 2017.

...the world's last great unprotected stands of old-growth *Eucalyptus regnans* are being reduced to piles of smouldering ash. Over 85 per cent of Tasmania's old-growth *regnans* forests are gone, and it is estimated that fewer than 13,000 hectares of these extraordinary trees remain in their old-growth form. Almost half of them are to be clearfelled...The hellish landscape that results from clearfelling—akin to a Great War battlefield—is generally turned into large monocultural plantations of either radiata pine or *Eucalyptus nitens*, sustained by such a heavy program of fertilisers and pesticides that water sources for some local communities have been contaminated by Atrazine, a controversial herbicide linked with cancer and banned in much of Europe.[7]

Flanagan also details the large number of protected species—wombats, bettongs, potoroos and others—that die in large numbers as a result of this pesticide use; and makes clear that it's not just about jobs, nor even money. At the time he wrote that essay, logging contracts were being slashed to offset the decline in woodchip sales.

One of the species we'll lose if the mountain ash forests collapse is the Leadbeater's possum. By the time of the Black Friday fires in 1939, the tiny marsupial was thought to be extinct. In 1961, a colony was discovered near Marysville in

---

7   'Out of Control: the tragedy of Tasmania's forests', Richard Flanagan, *Monthly*, May 2007.

Victoria. The combination of forty-year-old regrowth (for food) and large dead trees left still standing after the fires (for shelter and nesting) encouraged the Leadbeater's possum population to reach a peak of about 7500 in the early 1980s. Then in February 2009 the Black Saturday bushfires destroyed forty-three per cent of possum habitats and the wild population of the possum halved with it. The tiny possum doesn't live only in mountain ash, but another favoured habitat, the snow gum (*Eucalyptus pauciflora*), is also under threat. The increasing frequency of bushfires makes regeneration harder and takes out those seedlings that do manage to spring up.[8]

Under business-as-usual management, large, hollow-bearing trees will decline to less than one per hectare by 2067, leaving the Leadbeater's possum and some species of gliders and other marsupials with almost nowhere to live. Gliders have already disappeared from some of our national parks and are in dramatic decline in mountain ash forest around Australia.

I saw a greater glider, larger and more robust than a sugar glider or a Leadbeater's, one dark night in a national park east of Canberra. I remember the creamy glow of its underbelly soaring, the inelegant thud as it landed. The joy of, the miracle in seeing, such a rare and beautiful marsupial glide from treetop to treetop. There is much that broke my heart when researching the essays in this book. But it is this, our wanton destruction of the mountain ash and those that live in them, that has brought me closest to giving up hope.

---

8 'Recurring fires are threatening the iconic snow gum', Tom Fairman, Associate Professor Lauren Bennett and Dr Craig Nitschke, *Pursuit*, University of Melbourne.

*

So it is fair to say as I stand before Ada, arms held wide, that I am exactly the kind of person Richard Fortey cautions against. I leap to conclusions, faulty or otherwise. I drop to my knees, say a prayer, swear an oath: I will drive, I will wade, through fields laid waste by clearfelling, through ancient and perfect rainforest, to stand before you, my queen. I don't say this out loud of course, but I think it, in the hope she'll pick up my thoughts.

She does.

Ada rises above me. The wind rustles through her and the frogs croak in her, giving her voice. She holds a Leadbeater's possum in her hollow like an orb, she brandishes her branches as a sceptre, as a sword.

I honour you, I say. I pledge my allegiance to you, to this city—to our planet—of trees.

ACKNOWLEDGMENTS

Thank you to my wife, Virginia Murdoch. This project would literally not exist were it not for her support and adventurous spirit.

'Staying with the Trouble' was first published by *Australian Book Review* in May 2015 after winning the 2015 Calibre Essay Prize.

Sections of my writing about San Francisco were published as an essay entitled 'Gold rush' in *Overland* 221, Summer 2015.

Sections of 'Escape to Alcatraz' were published as an essay entitled 'Gardening at Alcatraz' in the *Monthly*, March 2016.

'Biyala Stories' was first published online, by *Griffith Review* in partnership with the Nature Conservancy Australia, in May 2017 after winning the 2015 Nature Writing Prize.

A version of 'Giant Sequoia' was published as 'How to Draw a Tree' in *Griffith Review*, February 2019.

Sections of this book were written while an Artist-in-Residence at the Bundanon Trust in 2017.

Tree enthusiasts, scientists and writers who were particularly generous with their learning include Saul Cunningham, Rebecca Giggs, Ashley Hay, Matthew Colloff, David Lindenmayer, Peter Scott.

Family members who shared details of our family history with me include Bill Cunningham, Meg L'estrange, Carol Tobin, Sari Wawn.

Many of my friends, whether they knew it or not, supported this project. They include Donica Bettanin, James Bradley, Janice Campbell, Griff Clemens, Ann Clemenza, Julie Franklin, Carolyn Fraser, Jane Gleeson-White, Andre Govberg, Anna Grace Hopkins, Lorna Hendry, Judy Horacek, Dai Hovey, Greg Hunt, Kerry Gardiner, Amber Jamieson, Fiona McGregor, Lucy Morrison, David Mow, Peta Murray, Joseph Pearson, Francesca Rendle-Short, Estelle Tang, Deb Verhoeven, Dianna Wells and WH Chong. I can't list you all here, but thanks too to those who have sent me trees for posting as #treeoftheday over the years. Nor can I list all who have walked and travelled with me over the last few years, but I thank you also.

Thank you to the team at Text, most particularly Mandy Brett and WH Chong.

All errors, of course, remain my own.

This book is dedicated to the memory of:
John Cunningham, 1946–2016
Georgia Blain, 1964–2016
Peter Nicholls, 1939–2018

BIBLIOGRAPHY

Books

Bearbrass, Robyn Annear, Black Inc., 2005.

1835, James Boyce, Black Inc., 2013.

Silent Spring, Rachel Carson, 1962 (www.newyorker.com/
magazine/1962/06/16/silent-spring-part-1).

*Flooded Forest and Desert Creek: Ecology and History of the River Red
Gum*, Matthew Colloff, CSIRO Publishing, 2014.

Native Trees and Shrubs of South-eastern Australia, Leon Costermans,
Reed New Holland, 2009.

The Art of Wandering: The Writer as Walker, Merlin Coverley, Old
Castle Books, 2012.

Ginkgo: The Tree that Time Forgot, Sir Peter Crane, Yale University
Press, 2013.

Warning: The Story of Cyclone Tracy, Sophie Cunningham, Text
Publishing, 2014.

Slouching Towards Bethlehem, Joan Didion, Farrar, Straus and
Giroux, 1968.

Trees in Paradise, Jared Farmer, W. W. Norton, 2013.

The Life and Adventures of William Buckley, edited and introduced by
Tim Flannery, Text Publishing, 2002.

Europe: A Natural History, Tim Flannery, Text Publishing, 2018.

Coyote America, Dan Flores, Basic Books, 2016.

Staying with the Trouble: Making Kin in the Chthulucene, Donna J. Haraway, Duke University Press, 2016.

Gum: The Story of Eucalypts and Their Champions, Ashley Hay, Duffy & Snellgrove, 2002.

The New York Nobody Knows: Walking 6000 Miles in the City, William B. Helmreich, Princeton University Press, 2013.

Ghosting William Buckley, Barry Hill, William Heinemann, 1993.

Cool Gray City of Love: 49 Views of San Francisco, Gary Kamiya, Bloomsbury USA, 2013.

'Us and Them: On the Importance of Animals', *Quarterly Essay*, Anna Krien, Black Inc., 2012.

Feral, George Monbiot, Penguin Books, 2013.

'Icelandic Journals', *Collected Works of William Morris*, William Morris, vol. 8, 1911.

'The Big Trees', *The Yosemite*, John Muir, 1912.

Story about Feeling, Bill Neidjie and Keith Taylor, Magabala Books, 1989.

The Botany of Desire, Michael Pollan, Random House, 2001.

The Place for a Village, Gary Presland, Museum Victoria Publishing, 2008.

First People, Gary Presland, Museum Victoria Publishing, 2010.

Burning Bush: A Fire History of Australia, Stephen Pyne, Weyerhaeuser Environmental Books, 1998.

Wild Dog Dreaming: Love and Extinction, Deborah Bird Rose, University of Virginia Press, 2011.

Wanderlust: A History of Walking, Rebecca Solnit, Penguin Books, 2001.

Should Trees Have Standing? Law, Morality, and the Environment, Christopher D. Stone, W. Kaufman, 1974.

The Trees of San Francisco: Second Edition, Mike Sullivan, Wilderness Press, 2013.

Australian Pictures Drawn with Pen and Pencil, Howard Willoughby,

Religious Tract Society, London, 1886.

The Dog Fence, James Woodford, Text Publishing, 2003.

Articles

'Fears for the future of Australia's koalas', *RN Breakfast*, ABC, December 14, 2018.

'Extinction: A Matter of Life and Death?', *The Philosopher's Zone*, ABC, November 21, 2014.

'The Lost Poetry of the Angel Island Detention Center', Beenish Ahmed, *New Yorker*, February 22, 2017.

'WW III Is Well Underway, Says Environmentalist Bill McKibben', Arpan Bhattacharyya, *Big Think*, September 11, 2016.

'Greenland Ice Melt Could Push Atlantic Circulation to Collapse', Rebecca Boyle, *Hakai Magazine*, January 3, 2017.

'An Ocean and an Instant', James Bradley, *Sydney Review of Books*, August 21, 2018.

'The Plant Men of Alcatraz', Patricia Leigh Brown, *New York Times*, June 21, 2001.

'Senate launches inquiry into threatened species "extinction crisis"', Lisa Cox, *Guardian*, June 27, 2018.

'A week in the life of P-22, the big cat who shares Griffith Park with millions of people', Thomas Curwen, *Los Angeles Times*, February 8, 2017.

'Which is the world's most biodiverse city?', Feike De Jong, *Guardian*, July 3, 2017.

'The Whispering Leaves of the Hiroshima Ginkgo Trees', Ariel Dorfman, *New York Times*, August 4, 2017.

'Recurring fires are threatening the iconic snow gum', Tom Fairman, Associate Professor Lauren Bennett and Dr Craig Nitschke, *Pursuit*, University of Melbourne.

'California Burning', William Finnegan, *New York Review of Books*, vol. 65, no. 13, August 16, 2018.

'Out of Control: the tragedy of Tasmania's forests', Richard Flanagan, *Monthly*, May 2007.

'Unmourned death of a sole survivor', Tim Flannery, *Sydney Morning Herald,* November 17, 2012.

'Whale Fall', Rebecca Giggs, *The Best Australian Essays 2016*, Black Inc., 2016. Originally published in Sigrid Rausing (ed.), *Granta Magazine*, issue 133, 'What Have We Done', December, 2015.

'It's only natural: the push to give rivers, mountains and forests legal rights', Jane Gleeson-White, *Guardian*, April 1, 2018.

'Do trees talk to each other', Richard Grant, *Smithsonian Magazine*, March, 2018.

'Remembering Aboriginal Fitzroy', Alick Jackomos, quoted in aboriginalhistoryofyarra.com.au

'Paper Tiger', Brooke Jarvis, *New Yorker*, July 2, 2018.

'The Scandal at the Zoo', Mitch Keller, *New York Times*, August 6, 2006.

'Why Are Some Depressed, Others Resilient? Scientists Home in on One Part of the Brain', Meeri Kim, *Washington Post*, June 5, 2014.

'Letter from Florida: The Siege of Miami', Elizabeth Kolbert, *New Yorker*, December 21 & 28, 2015.

'The Voice of the Natural World', Bernie Krause, TED Talk, August 27, 2014.

'Global Decline in Large Old Trees', David B. Lindenmayer, William F. Laurance, Jerry F. Franklin, sciencemag.com, December 6, 2012.

'The ecology, distribution, conservation and management of large old trecs', David B. Lindenmayer and William F. Laurance, *Biol. Rev.* (2017), 92, pp. 1434–58. 1434 doi: 10.1111/brv.12290.

'Conserving large old trees as small natural features', David B. Lindenmayer, *Biological Conservation*, 211 (2017) 51–9.

'Hidden collapse is driven by fire and logging in a sociological forest ecosystem', David B. Lindenmayer and Chloe Sato, *PNAS*, vol. 115, May 15, 2018.

'Leaving Time at the Zoo', Liam Mannix, *Age*, December 16, 2018.

'"Reading" the Leichhardt, Landsborough and Gregory Explorer Trees of Northern Australia', Richard J. Martin, *Cultural Studies Review*, vol. 19, no. 2, September, 2013, pp. 216–36.

'In the Land of the Giants', Jon Mooallem, *New York Times*, March 23, 2017.

'Queenie's Last Ride', Mary O'Brien, *Age*, August 9, 2006.

'Shooting an Elephant', George Orwell, 1936.

'Gentrification Spreads an Upheaval in San Francisco's Mission District', Carol Pogash, *New York Times*, May 22, 2015.

'The Concrete Jungle', David Quammen, *New York Review of Books*, November 8, 2018.

'How Many Trees Are Enough? Tree Death and the Urban Canopy', Lara A. Roman, *Scenario 04: Building the Urban Forest*, Spring, 2014.

'The Elephant as a Person', Don Ross, *Aeon*, October 24, 2018.

'Little girl, rose still in hand, found in coffin beneath SF home', Steve Rubenstein, *San Francisco Chronicle*, May 25, 2016.

'Syme, George Alexander (1822–1894)', C. E. Sayers, *Australian Dictionary of Biography*, vol. 6, MUP, 1976.

'Old-growth trees to be "woodchipped, wasted" under specialty timber access plan', Rhiannon Shine, *ABC News*, August 4, 2017.

'Australia's endangered forests are being "stolen" and sold in hardware and office stores', Michael Slezak and Penny Timms, ABC News, November 21, 2018.

'Bong Su is dead, broken by cramped and impoverished zoo conditions', Peter Stroud, *Sydney Morning Herald*, October 13, 2017.

'Giants in the Face of Drought', Thayer Walker, *Atlantic,* November 27, 2016.

'The Woman Who Walked 10,000 Miles (No Exaggeration) in Three Years', Elizabeth Weil, *New York Times*, September 25, 2014.

'The Last Days of the Blue-Blood Harvest', Sarah Zhang, *Atlantic*, May 9, 2018.

PhDs and Reports

Submission to Victorian Environmental Assessment Council (VEAC) on Yorta Yorta Connections with River Red Gum forest on public land in Study Region, Dr Wayne Atkinson, University of Melbourne, June 13, 2005.

Federal Court of Australia, *Members of the Yorta Yorta Aboriginal Community v Victoria & Ors*, [1998] FCA 1606 (December 18, 1998).

Wurundjeri Tribe Land and Compensation Council, quoted in 'Indigenous Cultural Heritage and History within the Metropolitan Melbourne Investigation Area', A report to the Victorian Environmental Assessment Council, Dr Shaun Canning and Dr Frances Thiele, February, 2010, p. 23.

'Quarantine Station North Head 1900–1984: A history of place', Carmel Patricia Kelleher MA. Submitted in total fulfilment of the requirements of Doctor of Philosophy May, 2014, Department of Modern History, Politics and International Relations, Macquarie University.

Trustees Report 1905 (DOC/15/4134), National Museum of Victoria Zoological Department Report, Museums Victoria Archives, Vol/143; DOC/15/4700, p. 28.

Trustees Report 1923 (DOC/15/4134), National Museum of Victoria Zoological Department Report, Museums Victoria Archives, Vol/143; DOC/15/4700, p. 17.

Websites

australianwildlife.org

daao.org.au

emelbourne.net.au

glacierguides.is

italiannotes.com/pruning-olive-trees/

melbourneurbanforestvisual.com.au

melbourne.vic.gov.au/urbanforest

senseable.mit.edu